THE
ARTI
YEA

the
ARTFUL
YEAR

CELEBRATING THE SEASONS AND HOLIDAYS
WITH FAMILY ARTS AND CRAFTS

JEAN VAN'T HUL

ROOST
BOOKS

Boston & London | 2015

ROOST BOOKS
An imprint of Shambhala Publications, Inc.
Horticultural Hall
300 Massachusetts Avenue
Boston, Massachusetts 02115
roostbooks.com

9 8 7 6 5 4 3 2 1

First Edition
Printed in U.S.A.

♾ This edition is printed on acid-free paper that meets the American National Standards Institute z39.48 Standard.
♻ Shambhala Publications makes every effort to print on recycled paper. For more information please visit www.shambhala.com.

Distributed in the United States by Penguin Random House LLC and in Canada by Random House of Canada Ltd

Designed by Daniel Urban-Brown

LIBRARY OF CONGRESS CATALOGING-IN-PUBLICATION DATA

Van't Hul, Jean.
The artful year: celebrating the seasons & holidays with family arts and crafts / Jean Van't Hul.—First edition.
Pages   cm
Includes bibliographical references and index.
ISBN 978-1-61180-149-1 (alk. paper)
1. Handicraft. 2. Holiday decorations. 3. Family recreation. 4. Seasonal cooking. I. Title.
TT157.V2855 2015
745.594'16—dc23
2013048889

To families celebrating together!

CONTENTS

INTRODUCTION

Celebrating an Artful Year with Children

The art of mothering is to teach the art of living to children.
—ELAINE HEFFNER

IN OUR HOME, we celebrate the seasons and holidays through art, crafts, and cooking together. We mix the familiar (gingerbread cookies) with the unique and creative (stained glass garlands), and we're always trying out new ideas and combinations.

Celebrating the seasons and holidays is a traditional way to embrace creativity together as a family, but it's also much more: engaging in arts and crafts as a family is a fun way of decorating, preparing for, and learning about the holidays we celebrate while cultivating creativity and family bonds.

Instead of buying all of our decorations and materials, we prefer to take the time to make our holidays more fun and meaningful by doing at least some of the preparations ourselves. The rewards? Memories and mementos, creative growth in our children and ourselves, and lots of fun!

Art is often considered a solitary pursuit (although it is actually quite enjoyable to do with others), but crafting is traditionally done together (think quilting bees and sewing circles, abuzz with conversation as participants create together or side by side). I think of seasonal and holiday crafts and cooking as wonderful excuses to work with others toward a shared goal, with each member participating at his or her own level. The baby in the high chair can bang spoons while watching and listening, the toddler can help mix, the preschooler can measure out the dried cranberries, the older child can help read the recipe and gather ingredients, and the parents can both supervise (if needed) and help create. And at the end, we have fresh-baked oatmeal-cranberry cookies that we can sit down and enjoy together. There is more savoring, bonding, learning, and memory making in this creative process than when we come home and pop open a box of store-bought cookies. Not that we won't do that, too, but the family connections in the first scenario are treasured and definitely worth making an extra effort for.

In the past, families often created and connected more naturally. But now, with the fast pace of modern life, overscheduled families, and stores that sell every possible holiday item, we are hard-pressed to find time together. We need to be more deliberate about making this happen.

This is a book for families. When we become parents, we want to create special celebrations for our children. Although we ourselves stopped trick-or-treating and decorating Easter eggs as young adults, likely we will plunge back into the spirit of the holidays with enthusiasm when we have children of our own. We want to pass on cultural traditions to our kids, and we want to celebrate *with* them.

The crafts, activities, and recipes you'll find within these pages can be enjoyed by any family, no matter the size, ages, or stages of life. Many of the activities are easily adaptable. Families with younger children, just figuring out which traditions to welcome into their lives, may need to temper their enthusiasm according to the needs of babies and toddlers. Older children can do more themselves, needing little more than guidance and encouragement. But even if your child *can* do something on his or her own, I encourage you to engage in these activities together as a family, building relationships and traditions in the process.

We are so harried as parents, trying to juggle the impossible (fulfill our dreams, earn a living, build a career, raise children, navigate the modern world) and at the same time teach the art of living (well) to our children. We do the best we can with the resources, traditions, and energy we have at our disposal. I believe "the best we can" includes celebrating the cycles of life in meaningful ways with our children, funneling the enthusiasm and excitement for the holidays into family harmony and special learning experiences.

We all have the same amount of time—at the end of the year we have each just "spent" a year. Why not make it an artful year? In doing so, we

- cultivate a family environment, make memories, and form stronger family bonds while crafting, baking, and celebrating;
- pass on cultural traditions while continuing to evolve and try new things;
- nurture creativity, arguably the most important skill of the twenty-first century;
- consciously enjoy and celebrate all that makes each season and holiday unique;
- raise children who can connect with others and with nature, who know how to live life fully, and who can in turn pass on *their* favorite traditions to *their* children.

I embrace the cycle of the year and use my own creativity to tease out the artfulness of the season and of my family. I seek ways to celebrate that are easy and enjoyable for everyone to do together, with the goal of growing creatively as we celebrate and connect. *That's me.*

You are your own best expert on your family traditions as you blend old and new and take your own family year to new artful heights. Anything and everything can be artful, creative, celebrated.

Celebrating 101

When we plan celebrations, many of us think of a party. But we can also celebrate by noticing, sharing, capturing, and creating.

The simple act of noticing and appreciating can be an act of celebration. We celebrate autumn when we go on a fall foliage drive. We celebrate spring with a nature walk to see the crab apple in bloom and new life unfurling around us. It's perhaps the simplest way to celebrate, but really noticing is at the heart of any celebration.

We take it a step further when we share what we observe with those close to us. We take home the most brilliant red and yellow leaves from under the maple tree to show to our family. Or we pass the binoculars to a friend and point out the bird's nest high up in the tree.

Collecting or "capturing" something is another way to celebrate it. We do this when we photograph a child leaping through the sprinkler on a hot summer day—we celebrate the moment and preserve it. We celebrate autumn when gathering acorns and pinecones for our fall nature table. We celebrate Christmas when we draw Santa Claus or the Nativity scene from our imagination. When we choose apple or pumpkin for our cooking, we are capturing the flavors of the season. When we pick daffodils for our windowsill, we are reveling in spring.

And we celebrate through the act of creation as well—whether it's baking a favorite birthday cake, decorating Easter eggs, or making Christmas ornaments out of salt dough.

The next time you prepare to celebrate a season or holiday, think beyond the party. Notice. Share. Capture. Create.

Considering Traditions

Many of our ideas about seasonal and holiday celebrations are bound by tradition. By definition, traditions are long-established patterns and rituals that are handed down from generation to generation, and we all cherish some of these from our childhoods. Yet they don't all have to be the same every year. We can modify or discard traditions that are no longer working for our families and even audition a few new ideas each season.

We can and should take a deliberate approach to the cycle of our family year and the traditions we develop together. As we do this, we consider the values we hope to instill in our children. (For me, those values are to be resourceful and creative, slow down, celebrate the life around us, create together as a family, experience and enjoy the seasonal changes, and recognize the beauty in nature and in the handmade.) We can be mindful of how we connect with each other, our past, the natural world, and humankind.

When evaluating or forming seasonal and holiday traditions, I like to keep in mind the old English wedding rhyme "something old, something new, something borrowed, something blue." Something old can, of course, refer to a tradition that has been passed down to us from previous generations. Something new can be the creativity we use as we celebrate the season, make things, and introduce new traditions. Something borrowed can be ideas brought in from the cultures represented by each side of the family as well as anything we see around us (Pinterest, anyone?) that we want to try. Something blue can represent the colors, images, and scents of the season.

While this wedding rhyme had me scrambling to find the (seemingly) arbitrary blue item when I got married, I like its basic wisdom. Take a bit of tradition, give it a novel twist and shape it to fit your family, and combine it with all that makes a season unique.

How to Use This Book

As you begin reading *The Artful Year,* choose your season and browse through the activities, recipes, and photos. Don't expect to do everything in the book. Earmark those that speak to you. Try a couple now, save a couple for next year. Some will become family traditions that you do year after year, some you may try just once, and others may inspire your own ideas or adaptations.

As you craft and cook with children, be attentive to their skills, ages, and developmental stages. Use your judgment in deciding what they can do on their own, what you will help them with, and which steps you might want to do yourself.

Most of the materials mentioned are easily found at your local craft store. However, I've provided a resources section at the back of the book for any that might be harder to locate (liquid watercolors and BioColor paint, for example).

The act of making is as important as enjoying the finished product, whether it is a drawing, a Halloween decoration, or chicken noodle soup. With art, especially children's art, the process is more important than the finished product. The exploration of materials, techniques, tools, ability, and interests trumps all. There may not even *be* a finished product (think finger painting on a table or an ice sculpture than melts away). With crafts, however, there is the expectation that if we're sitting down to create starry Christmas ornaments out of Popsicle sticks, there will, in fact, be a wood star of some sort at the end that we can hang on our tree. So the end product is a bit more specific than with art. But there is still a process to be enjoyed. I like to think of this as the zen of crafting. Here are some tips for approaching the crafts in this book:

Use materials that you love and love your materials. Soak in the paint colors, run your fingertips over the lace, inhale deeply the aroma of the apples. Use all of your senses to connect with the materials at hand.

Embrace the process and take your time. It's not a race to finish the craft you are working on. Instead, slow down and really experience and enjoy the materials, the process, and the company.

See the beauty and the humanity in imperfection. Simply continue creating. If you make something that you deem a mistake, decide how to move forward—keep it, transform it, or start over. It's really not a big deal.

Learn as you create. Continue to evolve both yourself and your craft.

Enjoy an Artful Year

When we celebrate the seasons (and the holidays so closely tied to them), we celebrate the cycle of life as well as our passage through time here on Earth. It is human nature to connect with those close to us as we celebrate life's events, including the seasons. Yet we need to be more intentional than ever as we carve out quality time together, celebrate in meaningful ways, build traditions and memories,

and create stronger families. It's not about doing more. It's about making choices, fostering creativity, and building family connection. Celebrating the seasons and holidays together is a wonderful way to do just that.

I hope you will join me in crafting and celebrating around the year!

ACTIVITIES FOR ALL SEASONS

The seasons are what
a symphony ought to be:
four perfect movements
in harmony with each other.

—ARTHUR RUBINSTEIN

ACTIVITIES

CELEBRATING EVERY SEASON

NATURE'S SEASONAL CYCLES continually surprise and inspire us all, young and old, but they are all the more exhilarating when witnessed with and through the eyes of a child. Seasonal changes are ideal for introducing children to visual arts and natural science, both of which begin with observation. As spring approaches, we delight in the unfurling of tiny leaves and fragrant blossoms. In summer a frenzied flora and fauna work hard, both competitively and harmoniously, to live out the best of the warm days and complete their life cycles. With autumn, the world experiences a beautiful death—a decay made so lovely that we can't help but fall for it anew each year. Winter returns with chilly dormancy, balanced by a warm indoor flurry of crafting, baking, holidays, and celebrations.

In my home we celebrate the cycles of the year by surrounding ourselves with the colors of the seasons, the flavors we mix up in the kitchen, beautiful seasonal picture books that capture the imagination and complement the mood, and the crafts we create, rotating and recycling as the seasons switch gears. Some crafts and activities are so exclusive or perfectly suited to the season that we celebrate them solely at that time of the year. Pumpkins. Candy canes. Easter eggs. Others are flexible favorites that can be enjoyed anytime, modified for each season as appropriate. Think playdough, scented and colored to match the season; suncatchers using natural materials; and drawing activities where any theme is fair game.

This is a chapter of just such flexible favorites that we find ourselves turning to again and again and simply adapting to the season at hand.

Exploring Nature

Observing and learning about the natural world as it morphs through the year form the foundation for our understanding of the cycle of the seasons. Young or old, when we take the time and let ourselves truly see—and young children, with their natural curiosity and lack of filters, are great companions for this endeavor—we will find miracles, surprises, and astounding beauty in the smallest nooks and crannies as well as in the grandest of vistas. Inspired by the ever-changing, ever-cycling natural world, my family and I take seasonal nature walks or scavenger hunts and later incorporate the treasures we find into our creative activities, or we display them on our nature table.

NATURE OBSERVATION AND COLLECTION WALK

Take nature walks year-round to observe the changes around you and to collect tokens of the season for your nature table (see page 11) or for arts and crafts projects.

MATERIALS

Big pockets and a basket or bag for holding the nature treasures you find
Camera or sketchbook and pencil for capturing images and ideas (optional)

INSTRUCTIONS

1. Take your nature walk close to home (backyard or neighborhood) or farther afield (take a drive to the countryside or go for a hike in the woods).

2. Explore and observe while you walk. Slow down and really look. See if you can spot the mushrooms half hidden among the leaves, the little grasshopper or snail, the shy birds hiding in the brush.

3. Collect treasures for your nature table or crafting, including leaves, flowers, rocks, acorns, shells, pinecones, seedpods, and more. (Make sure it's okay to collect where you are; it might not be permitted at an arboretum, for example.)

OBSERVING WILDLIFE

Growing up in rural Oregon with a naturalist for a mother, my siblings and I were introduced early to the wonders of wildlife of all kinds. Mom went into raptures over pileated woodpecker sightings, I brought a black widow spider for show-and-tell as a kindergartener (the teacher was *not* pleased), my sister was always the first to see the elusive deer at dawn and dusk, and my brother kept a baby possum on his shoulder. While you shouldn't feed or adopt wild animals, for many reasons (a memo my brother didn't get when choosing to care for the orphaned possum), observing insects, birds, and mammals is rewarding and educational.

BIRDS

Birds are wonderfully rewarding to observe and easy to attract around your house with feeders, birdbaths, birdhouses, and native plants. You can attach special feeders to your window with suction cups or install them in other ways within easy view of some of your main windows. (We especially love being able to watch the birds at our thistle and hummingbird feeders from our dining table.)

In the spring, you can encourage nesting by putting out cotton batting, string, and other materials they can use in building their nests.

Keep a bird guide handy and look up the birds you spot. We like *The Sibley Guide to Birds* by David Allen Sibley, but there are also many other well-respected bird guides to choose from. You can also learn more about birds by reading books such as *An Egg Is Quiet* by Diana Hutts Aston and *Crinkleroot's Guide to Knowing the Birds* by Jim Arnosky.

Start a feather collection. My older daughter has a box full of feathers—some local, some sent to her by Grandma, three thousand miles away.

Providing food and cover in the form of native plants is an especially helpful and effective way to attract birds. Unlike modern hybrids, native plants have been around for thousands of years and therefore attract local populations of birds, insects, and other wildlife. Some animals depend on them, and because they are suited to your locale, they often require little care. You can get native plant suggestions from botanical gardens, arboretums, local birder groups, and local chapters of the Native Plant Society.

INSECTS AND OTHER INVERTEBRATES

Keep a butterfly and bug watch to see how many different kinds live in your yard or neighborhood.

See how close you can get (be quiet and use slow movements) to a butterfly, beetle, spider, or praying mantis and how much detail you can observe. Can you draw it in a nature journal? Or look it up in an insect field guide?

Use a magnifying glass for roly-polies (pill bugs), worms, caterpillars, and others that don't move quickly.

If you catch a butterfly or a firefly and put it in a jar for close observation, make sure to add airholes at the top and to release it within an hour.

The dead, brown flower stalks in your garden can provide bug homes in the cold months. If you dislike leaving the unsightly stalks over winter, you can tie neat bundles of them with jute twine and stand them up at the back of your garden: insect apartment houses.

MAMMALS AND TRACKS

Depending on where you live, you may regularly see rabbits, raccoons, beavers, possums, groundhogs, deer, elk, and even bear. Or you may see them only when you visit your local nature center or zoo. Either way, make a point to learn more about the mammals around you through observation and reading. Are the animals nocturnal or diurnal? What kinds of food do they prefer? What are their habitats? Do they hibernate during the winter? What are their seasonal habits?

Subscribe to a wildlife publication aimed at children, such as *National Geographic* (*Kids* or *Little Kids*, depending on your child's age), *Ranger Rick* and *Ranger Rick Jr.*, *Click*, and *Zoobooks*.

You can learn a lot about animals from their tracks. On a camping trip, take a slow tour around your tent in the morning, with an eye for tracks made during the night. How close did an animal get? Do you know (can you guess?) what kind of animal it was? Was it alone or not? To learn more about animal tracks, read *Tracks, Scats, and Signs* by Leslie Dendy or *Wild Tracks! A Guide to Nature's Footprints* by Jim Arnosky.

SPRING

Observe: birds building nests and carrying materials back and forth in their beaks, ducklings following closely behind their mother, fuzzy chicks cheeping, knock-kneed foals, and trees changing daily—flower and leaf buds bursting open and growing larger by the day, colors deepening as the season progresses

Listen: birdsong heralding the return of warm weather, rain falling (how does it sound on the roof? on the grass? in the leafy tree canopy? on the car? on the umbrella?)

Smell: the earth after a rain, the heady fragrance of a lilac in full bloom

Taste: the sharp taste of fresh greens, oniony chives chopped into an omelet, the first juicy strawberries straight off the plant, rhubarb baked sweet and tangy in a flaky piecrust

Feel: the splash through a mud puddle, the fuzzy chick cupped gently in your palms, a hole in the garden soil scooped out with bare hands, the pussy willow on your fingertip, the warmth of the sun on your skin when the air is still cool

Collect: fiddlehead ferns to sauté, flowers for a bouquet or to press for crafts, eggshell fragments under birds' nests

SUMMER

Observe: butterflies sipping nectar from purple coneflowers and phlox, bees busy pollinating the plant world, ants marching ceaselessly, dandelion fluff scattering on a wish, all the colors of the rainbow represented in the flowers in bloom, and hummingbirds hovering, diving at each other, and (rarely) alighting on a branch

Listen: birdsong as the earliest and gentlest of alarm clocks, thunderstorms, the excitement at baseball games, lawn mowers across the neighborhood, the loud buzzing of cicadas, the annoying hum of mosquitoes

Smell: freshly mown grass, mint crushed between your fingers, salty sea air

Taste: watermelon, juicy sweet cherries, sun-ripened tomatoes paired with fresh mozzarella and basil, fresh blueberries eaten by the handful, creamy cold vanilla ice cream

Feel: warm summer rain, grass and shifting sand under bare feet, the heat of the sun

Collect: seashells, sea glass, driftwood, special rocks, animal tracks (captured as a photograph or plaster cast), the shed skin of a snake or cicada

AUTUMN

Observe: trees changing their garb at different rates into different colors, leaves dancing through the air with every gust of wind, squirrels on a mission to collect nuts, spiderwebs woven overnight and glistening with morning dew

Listen: wind whistling, leaves crunching dry underfoot, crickets chirring, the "whoo-whoo" of an owl at dusk

Smell: pumpkin pie spices, dry dusty leaves, and earthy decay

Taste: crisp sweet apples, fresh-baked pumpkin muffins, salty roasted pumpkin seeds, hot mulled cider, meaty walnuts

Feel: the thick layer of a sweater after a summer of bare arms, leaves crumbling between fingers, the warmth of a bonfire on face and hands

Collect: acorns, autumn leaves, pinecones, seedpods

WINTER

Observe: birds on the feeders or scavenging the remains of seeds and dried berries from the garden, icicles reaching down from the eaves, frost patterns across the windowpane, snow falling, flickering candlelight, footprints and animal tracks in the snow

Listen: the crunch of snow underfoot, the quiet after a snowstorm, Christmas carols, the crackling of a fire in the fireplace

Smell: the wonderful fragrance of a fresh Christmas tree, cookies baking in the oven, yeasty bread rising

Taste: peppermint candy canes, tangy cranberry sauce paired with savory turkey, hot chocolate after sledding

Feel: the snow giving way as you swing your arms and legs wide in a snow angel, the steamy warmth when coming in from the cold, the cozy comfort of being inside while a winter storm rages outside

Collect: snowflakes on black construction paper, the longest icicles

OUR FAVORITE BOOKS ABOUT THE FOUR SEASONS

Seasons by Anne Crausaz
The Seasons of Arnold's Apple Tree by Gail Gibbons
Our Seasons by Ranida T. McKneally
A Time to Keep: The Tasha Tudor Book of Holidays by Tasha Tudor

NATURE TABLES

Display the elements and mementos of the season that you find on your nature walks, along with your seasonal arts and crafts—at least the smaller ones. A special table or shelf that is at child level yet not needed for regular household use is ideal. Keep a magnifying glass handy for viewing details.

SPRING NATURE-TABLE IDEAS

Flowers
Pussy willows
Potted bulbs
A pretend bird's nest
Robin's egg fragments

Forsythia stems to force indoors (that is, to speed up their blooming by putting them in water inside where the air is warm)

Dyed eggs (see page 54)

Pretend eggs, purchased or handmade

Animal figurines (lambs, chicks, foals, ducklings)

Leafy branch

Drawings or paintings of eggs, nests, birds, and flowers

People figurines

Play silks or fabric in pastel colors

SUMMER NATURE-TABLE IDEAS

Flowers

Seashells

Sand

Sand-castings (see page 163)

Tree branch with green leaves

Drawings or paintings of suns, butterflies, fish

Animal and people figurines

Play silks or fabrics in bright colors

AUTUMN NATURE-TABLE IDEAS

Colorful fall leaves

Pinecones

Acorns

Pumpkins, squash, gourds

Jack-o'-lanterns (see pages 197–201)

Seedpods

Feathers

Drawings or paintings of leaves, pumpkins, squirrels, Halloween, harvest

Animal and people figurines

Play silks or fabric in oranges, reds, browns, or yellows

WINTER NATURE-TABLE IDEAS

Pine boughs
Pinecones
Potted bulbs
Rocks
Crystals
Drawings or paintings of snowmen, snow scenes, penguins
Paper snowflakes
Animal and people figurines
Play silks or fabrics in white, pale blue, gray

NATURE'S COLORS SCAVENGER HUNT

Take the opportunity to really notice the palette of the season with color-themed scavenger hunts.

PAINT CHIPS SCAVENGER HUNT
INSTRUCTIONS

Pick up some paint chips (color sample cards) in the colors of the season at the paint or hardware store, and see if you can match each color with items you find on your nature walks or around your backyard.

PHOTOGRAPHY SCAVENGER HUNT
INSTRUCTIONS

1. On a piece of paper, make a list of all the colors you'd like to find. In spring the list might include the colors of the flowers starting to bloom or the grass and leaves returning; in the fall, the list might include the colors of the turning leaves. Take a look at the colors emerging in your area.

2. Set out on a walk around the

backyard or on an excursion farther away (a botanical garden or a drive through the countryside) and observe the colors all around you while looking for those on your list.

3. Take photos of the colors that match your list. If desired, you can get prints made and create a collage or scrapbook with the seasonal colors and images.

1007-1C Powder Peach
For Best Results Tintable
Color Primer is Required (see back)

Crafts for Any Season

Some crafts are so loved, yet basic, that we like to do them around the year, simply adapting them to the season or holiday as appropriate or desired. This includes nature crafts, such as nature suncatchers, which we make all year-round, varying them with the leaves and flowers available at the time. And playdough, which my kids never get tired of. We enjoy mixing up new batches with the scents and colors of the season. Stones are popular with children as canvases for paint, and they easily inspire a number of seasonal craft projects.

PLAYDOUGH

Our favorite, basic playdough recipe is easily adapted for any season or holiday by varying the color and adding glitter, essential oils, or spices.

INGREDIENTS

5 cups water
2½ cups salt
2 tablespoons cream of tartar
Food coloring or liquid watercolor paint (not glitter liquid watercolors)
Large pot
8 tablespoons vegetable oil
5 cups all-purpose flour
Wooden or other strong spoon
Glitter (optional)
Essential oils (optional)

INSTRUCTIONS

1. Mix the water, salt, cream of tartar, and food coloring in a large pot.

2. Cook the mixture on medium-low heat, stirring regularly until it is hot.

3. Add the oil and mix.
4. Stir in the flour, 1 cup at a time, mixing between each addition with a wooden or other strong spoon.
5. Continue to mix until the playdough pulls away from the pan and is no longer sticky. Pinch it between your fingers to test it.
6. Place the dough on the counter, let it cool a bit, and then knead. *Note:* This is the time to add glitter or essential oils. Simply place the additions in a well in the center of the playdough, then knead the dough thoroughly to mix.
7. Store the dough in an airtight bag or other container at room temperature. It will keep for months.

SPRING

Make lavender playdough by adding a small amount of purple food coloring (or liquid watercolors) and a few drops of lavender essential oil to a batch of basic playdough. You can also add dried lavender and glitter, if you like. The lavender color and scent of this playdough make us think of spring. Use it to make flowers, nests, eggs, and birds.

SUMMER

Make a lemonade playdough by adding a small amount of yellow food coloring (or liquid watercolors) and a few drops of lemon essential oil to a batch of basic playdough. The fresh lemonade smell of this playdough makes it perfect for summer! Use it to create suns, cupcakes, and sea creatures.

AUTUMN

Make pumpkin pie playdough by adding small amounts of red and yellow food coloring (or orange liquid watercolors) and 2 tablespoons of Pumpkin Pie Spice Mix (see page 221) or cinnamon to a batch of basic playdough. Use this playdough to make jack-o'-lanterns (page 198), monsters (with googly eyes and pipe cleaners), or anything else.

WINTER

Make candy cane playdough by mixing two batches of basic playdough; add a small amount of red food coloring (or liquid watercolors) to one batch and leave the other white. Add some glitter and a few drops of peppermint essential oil to both. Make snakes from each color and twist them together for candy canes, or make Candy Cane Playdough Gifts (see page 259).

NATURE SUNCATCHERS

Flower petals and leaves are attached to transparent contact paper in these colorful suncatchers, which are great for dangling in a sunny window or on the porch. You can create all-over random patterns, circular mandalas, faces, or other images with this technique. Select bits of natural materials that are in keeping with the season. *Note:* Your flowers and leaves will lose some color over time. Use this as an opportunity for observation and discussion with your kids.

MATERIALS

Scissors
White paper plates (the thin, cheap kind work best)
Transparent contact paper (also called sticky-back plastic)
Flowers and leaves
Hole punch
Yarn or ribbon

INSTRUCTIONS

1. Cut the center out of your paper plate.
2. Fold a piece of contact paper in half and cut out a full circle that is ½"–1" larger than the hole in the paper plate. You should now have two circles of the same size.
3. Pull off the paper backing of one of your circles and adhere the contact paper to the back of the paper plate, sticky side facing the side you would eat from.
4. Press flower petals, small leaves, and leaf pieces to the sticky side of the contact paper, arranging them in any design desired
5. When you're satisfied with your design, press the second contact-paper circle over the arrangement, sticky side down, to sandwich them between the two pieces of contact paper.
6. Punch a hole through the paper plate at the top of your suncatcher.

Thread a length of yarn through the hole and tie it to form a loop.

7. Hang the suncatcher in the window and admire it when the sun shines through.

SPRING

Use new green leaves and ferns as well as spring flowers.

SUMMER

There is a kaleidoscope of flower colors to choose from now.

AUTUMN

Use chrysanthemum flowers and the vivid autumn leaves.

WINTER

Try the leaves of evergreens (or houseplants) and the blossoms from late-winter blooming shrubs such as witch hazel and forsythia.

NATURE STAINED GLASS WINDOWS

Be creative in the way you bring nature into your home. Not only can you have bouquets on your table, but you can also put flowers on your windows for a colorful but natural stained glass effect. See the seasonal variations for the Nature Suncatchers above for ideas here. *Note:* Your flowers and leaves will lose some color over time. Use this as an opportunity for observation and discussion with your kids.

MATERIALS

Scissors
Transparent contact paper (also called sticky-back plastic)

Tape
Flower petals and leaves

INSTRUCTIONS

1. Choose the window you'll use. A multipaned one is effective but not necessary.

2. Cut the contact paper into pieces to fit each pane. If you're using a window that doesn't have multiple panes, you can cut one or more large sheets of contact paper to span the width of the window or just do a small section.

3. Pull the paper backing off the contact paper and tape each piece, sticky-side up, to your table or work surface.

4. Arrange flower petals (not the whole flower unless they're very small and flat) and leaves, as desired, across each piece of contact paper, making sure to leave ample contact paper uncovered to stick to the window.

5. Remove the tape and adhere the sticky side of each stained glass panel to a windowpane. Continue until all panes are covered.

6. Stand back and admire the color of the flowers and leaves as the light shines through.

7. To remove your stained glass, simply peel the contact paper off the window. Use window cleaner or soap and water to remove any flower and leaf residue from the windows.

Same as for the Nature Suncatchers above.

MELTED-CRAYON SUNCATCHERS

Melted-crayon suncatchers are a favorite for hanging in the window. They can be made with any colors and cut into any shapes, perfect for adapting to different seasons and holidays. We especially enjoy using autumn leaves in the fall and shaping hearts around Valentine's Day.

MATERIALS

Cheese grater
Crayons
Bowls or muffin tin
Iron
Wax paper
Ironing board
Newsprint or any cheap paper, such as copy paper
Scissors
Hole punch
Yarn or string

INSTRUCTIONS

1. Grate the crayons, keeping the colors separate in bowls or muffin tin sections.
2. Preheat the iron on the cotton setting; make sure to turn off the steam.
3. Cut a length of wax paper. Fold it in half, making a crease at the center. Unfold it again and lay it out on your work surface.
4. Sprinkle grated crayons over one half of the wax paper. Fold the other half on top to cover the crayon.

5. Carefully set the wax paper sandwich on your ironing board between layers of newsprint (the newsprint will protect your iron from being damaged by the melting crayon). Iron the sandwich enough to melt the crayon.

6. Make as many as desired. Replace the newsprint as it gets oily and crayon covered.

7. Cut shapes out of the melted-crayon stained glass sheets. You can cut freehand or use a cookie cutter or a computer printout as a template.

8. Punch a hole through the top of each melted-crayon suncatcher. String yarn through the hole and tie the ends to create a loop to use for hanging the suncatcher in a sunny window.

SPRING

Colors: yellow, pink, light green, lavender
Shapes: birds, flowers, Easter eggs

SUMMER

Colors: blue, green, orange, yellow, fuchsia
Shapes: butterflies, flowers, sea creatures

AUTUMN

Colors: orange, red, gold, brown
Shapes: autumn leaves, pumpkins, jack-o'-lanterns, acorns

WINTER

Colors: red, white, green, silver, gold
Shapes: stars, hearts, snowflakes, pine trees

EMBROIDERY AROUND THE YEAR

Embroidery is a basic sewing activity that can be enjoyed at any level, from complete beginner to accomplished needleworker. We especially like to embroider holiday and seasonal themes as decorations and gifts.

MATERIALS

Embroidery hoop
Fabric of your choice (burlap, muslin, cotton, felt)

Scissors

Water-soluble marker (available at sewing and craft stores) or permanent Sharpie marker

Dropper (optional)

Rubbing alcohol (optional)

Embroidery floss

Embroidery needle

INSTRUCTIONS

1. Separate the two halves of the embroidery hoop and lay your fabric over the inner half. Press the outer embroidery hoop section over the fabric and the inner half, turning the screw to tighten the hoop. Pull the fabric taut as you tighten. Trim the fabric around the hoop, leaving a couple of inches.

2. Beginners may find it helpful to draw a simple design on their fabric and use the lines as sewing guides. If you want the lines to wash out, use a water-soluble marker. If you don't mind permanent lines or you like to incorporate generous amounts of drawing with a little bit of embroidery (as my four-year-old does), then use permanent Sharpie markers. *Note:* To create an interesting tie-dye effect while retaining your child's drawn lines, use a dropper to drip small amounts of rubbing alcohol over the Sharpie drawing and watch the color spread. Let the fabric dry before beginning embroidery.

3. Thread the needle with the desired color of embroidery floss, adding a double knot at the end. Poke the needle through the fabric, from the back to the front, and pull all the way through so that the knot rests against the back of the fabric.

4. Beginners will find it easiest to start with the basic running stitch, poking the needle and thread in and out along the design line, and having roughly the same amount of thread showing on the top as on the bottom. For those ready to try different stitches, you can search online for basic embroidery stitches or pick up a book, such as *Doodle Stitching: Fresh and Fun Embroidery for Beginners* by Aimee

Ray and *Sewing School: 21 Sewing Projects Kids Will Love to Make* by Amie Plumley and Andria Lisle.

5. As you get close to the end of a piece of thread, tie a double knot at the back of the fabric and cut off the extra thread. Thread a new length of embroidery floss onto the needle, add a knot, and poke the needle through, picking up where you left off. Continue embroidering until you are finished with your design, again adding a knot on the reverse to hold your stitches in place before cutting off the extra thread.

6. Display your embroidered design in the hoop (a few embroidery hoops grouped together on a wall look lovely). Alternatively, you can remove the fabric from the hoop and either frame it or sew it into a pillow or ornament.

SPRING

Fresh new leaves and flower buds, Easter themes, clouds and raindrops

SUMMER

Rainbows, flags, ocean waves, octopus, sun rays

AUTUMN

Acorns, squirrels, owls, Halloween themes

WINTER

Christmas themes, snowflakes, sled, polar bear, penguin, heart

DECORATED ROCKS

Affix small nature items or craft materials to rocks with Mod Podge or glue. These make novel seasonal centerpieces or additions to the nature table.

MATERIALS

Smooth pebbles and rocks
Paintbrush
Mod Podge or glue
Small nature items (dried leaves or flowers) or craft materials (fabric, decorative
    paper, washi tape, aluminum foil, or glitter)
Acrylic paint (optional)
Paint pens or Sharpies (optional)

INSTRUCTIONS

1. Wash your rocks and let them dry thoroughly before beginning.
2. Use a paintbrush to brush a layer of Mod Podge on the top of a rock.
3. Lay one or more of your nature items or craft materials faceup on the wet Mod Podge. (If you are using washi tape, there is no need for the Mod Podge. It will stick on its own.)
4. Brush another layer of Mod Podge over the surface, covering both the item and the top of the rock.
5. Repeat with as many rocks as desired.
6. Let the rocks dry completely, then use them for pretend play, a centerpiece, or a seasonal nature table.

SEASONAL VARIATIONS

SPRING

Pressed flowers

Fabric, paper, or washi tape in pastel colors and/or spring shapes

Paint oval rocks like Easter eggs

Paint oval rocks to resemble robins' eggs or other birds' eggs; use paint or
paint pens for speckles.

Wrap a rock in lace

SUMMER

Fabric, paper, or washi tape in bright colors and/or summer shapes

Paint or draw shells or sea creatures

Attach fabric or paper butterflies and flowers

Find larger rocks and paint doors, windows, roofs, and so forth on them;
nestle them in the garden for your fairies and elves

Doodle with a paint pen or Sharpie

AUTUMN

Small colorful autumn leaves, pressed and dried

Washi tape jack-o'-lanterns

Paint rounder rocks as pumpkins and jack-o'-lanterns and longer rocks as ghosts

Use paint pens or Sharpies to decorate a rock with a sugar skull motif (colorfully
decorated skulls are used in Mexico to celebrate the Day of the Dead)

Make rock monsters with the addition of googly eyes

WINTER

Add pretty little fabric hearts

Paint a heart or star on a rock with glue, then sprinkle it with glitter, shaking
off the excess

Make a rock snowman by carefully stacking three rocks and adding facial features and buttons with a paint pen or Sharpie

Doodle snowflakes on rocks with a white paint pen

POTATO PRINTING

Potato printing is a classic, simple craft for children that can be used to create cards, decorations, ornaments, abstract art, wrapping paper, or even an Advent calendar (see page 242).

MATERIALS

Sharp knife
Potatoes
Paint (tempera or BioColor, or water-based printing ink)
Plate or small bowl
Heavy paper or poster board
Glitter (optional)

INSTRUCTIONS

1. First, adults prepare the potato stamp by slicing a potato in half and then carving an image into the flat surface. Put an entire image on one potato half or carve components on separate potatoes, such as a tulip blossom on one, a stem on another, and a leaf on yet another.

2. Pour a thin layer of paint on the plate.

3. Your child can then press the potato stamp first in the paint, then firmly on the paper. Lift the potato to reveal the print.

4. Sprinkle glitter over the wet paint if desired.

5. Continue to print with additional images and colors as desired.

SPRING

Easter egg
Duckling
Fiddlehead
Daffodil
Tulip
Leaf

AUTUMN

Jack-o'-lantern
Pumpkin
Leaf
Bat
Ghost
Skull
Owl

SUMMER

Stars and stripes (for a flag)
Octopus
Seashell
Sun
Fish
Butterfly
Sailboat

WINTER

Stars
Heart
Ornament
Christmas tree
Simple snowflake
Wrapped gift
Angel

Art through the Seasons

Art is always appropriate, no matter the season. Drawing, painting, and other art activities are so open-ended that they can, of course, be done at any time of the year. And while there is no need to paint with orange just because it's October or draw the Easter bunny in March, you can adapt any art activity to the season or holiday with a choice of colors or images. Whether playing a family drawing game or creating salty watercolors, art is a fun way to incorporate the images and ideas around us, from bugs and cars to jack-o'-lanterns and valentine hearts.

SEASONAL OR HOLIDAY PASS-THE-DRAWING GAME

Draw with your child or in a group. This back-and-forth drawing technique makes for a fun bonding activity and also allows each participant both to inspire and to be inspired. The use of seasonal or holiday themes means that there is a ready mental library of images to draw from (you can also refer to the seasonal ideas below). With older children, you can experiment with a timer (1–2 minutes per turn, for example).

MATERIALS

Paper
Drawing tools, such as markers, colored pencils, or crayons

INSTRUCTIONS

1. Provide everyone with a sheet of paper and one or more drawing tools. Each person draws something related to the current season or holiday on his or her paper, then passes it to the left (if playing with three or more) or swaps papers (if two are playing).

2. Participants draw another image on

the paper they received, then pass or trade again.

3. Continue to draw and pass as long as desired and then share the completed works of art with each other.

SPRING

Easter themes, birds, the garden, the farm, spring, fairies

SUMMER

Flowers, the garden, the woodland, the beach, the ocean, insects, Independence Day–related themes

AUTUMN

Falling leaves, the woods, mushrooms, Halloween themes, haunted houses, Thanksgiving themes, turkeys

WINTER

Snowflakes, snowmen, Christmas themes, Christmas trees, the Nativity scene, Santa Claus, Valentine's Day themes

SIMON SAYS! DRAWING FOR EVERY SEASON

Players take turns giving the drawing instructions. This game is a variation of a Simon Says drawing game we like to play that can be done without the copy machine used here.

MATERIALS

Leaves, flowers, or other relatively flat seasonal items

Color copy machine (or your home printer, but if you don't have one, head to the copy shop for the first part of this activity)

Pens or markers (metallic Sharpies are especially effective over dark-colored areas)

INSTRUCTIONS

1. Assemble an assortment of leaves or seasonal items facedown on the copy machine glass and make a color copy. Repeat with other combinations. (Each person might like to arrange and copy his or her own selection.)

2. Sit down around a table with the other players, each with his or her own color copy and drawing tool.

3. Players take turns giving each other drawing instructions (zigzags, a squirrel, ten dots, a jack-o'-lantern, and so on). Each player draws on her or his color copy, on or around the images, to create a collage-like seasonal tableau.

4. Keep going around the circle a few times, making additions to your drawing, until the group is ready to stop.

5. Share the finished drawings.

SPRING

Copy: ferns, new leaves, flowers, dress-up bunny ears, a piece of lace, your hand, a puzzle piece

Draw: patterns, doodles, flowers, worms, rain, birds, a nest, Easter eggs, bunnies

SUMMER

Copy: flowers, leaves, a paper boat, shells, rocks, a postcard from the beach, a favorite animal figurine

Draw: patterns, doodles, fish, boats, shells, flowers, butterflies, bees, dragonflies

AUTUMN

Copy: autumn leaves, acorns, seedpods, a pumpkin drawing, a small model skeleton

Draw: patterns, doodles, jack-o'-lanterns, ghosts, scarecrows, squirrels, acorns, owls

WINTER

Copy: pine bough, rocks, a doily, a scrap of patterned fabric, a cookie cutter, a Christmas ornament

Draw: patterns, doodles, hearts, snowflakes, snowmen, mice, Christmas trees, stars, sleds

DOUBLE-DOODLE THROUGH THE SEASONS

This unique drawing activity uses both hands, making it especially good for developing both sides of the brain. Besides, it's fun! Any image that is mostly symmetrical is fair game for this drawing activity. Try a person or a face or any of the seasonal suggestions below. Of course, you can also simply create an abstract double-doodle.

MATERIALS

Tape (optional)
Paper
Two markers

INSTRUCTIONS

1. Tape the paper to the table to hold it in place (optional, but helpful for younger kids especially).
2. Holding a marker in each hand, place the tips side by side at the center of the paper. Begin drawing with both markers at the same time, creating a mirror image. For example, when the left marker is heading left to the edge of the paper, the right marker should be heading right to the other edge of the paper. When one marker is heading toward the center, the other should be as well.
3. Continue until your drawing is complete. This is just as fun for abstract doodling as it is for creating realistic images.

SPRING

Bunnies, Easter eggs, flowers

SUMMER

Butterflies, fish, flowers, starfish, suns, trees

AUTUMN

Jack-o'-lanterns, ghosts, skeletons, haunted house, leaves, owls, bats, spiders

WINTER

Snowmen, Christmas trees, stars, hearts, bears

SALTY WATERCOLORS AROUND THE YEAR

Salty watercolors are one of our very favorite art projects, and we're usually ready for another round every few months or so.

MATERIALS

Bottle of white glue
Card stock or watercolor paper
Salt (buy one or two cheap containers of table salt, such as Morton's)
Large baking dish or dishpan
Paintbrush
Liquid watercolors

INSTRUCTIONS

1. Draw a design or picture by squeezing glue onto the card stock. Younger children will likely make abstract designs; older ones may draw more realistic pictures.

2. Sprinkle the glue picture liberally with salt, tipping off the excess. This is best done over a large dish.

3. Dip a paintbrush into liquid watercolors, then touch it lightly to a salt-covered glue line. Watch as the paint travels along the line!

4. Continue with more paint and colors until the entire picture is painted as desired.

SEASONAL VARIATIONS

SPRING

Flowers, gardens, rabbits, chicks, Easter eggs, nests, birds

SUMMER

Frogs, bees, butterflies, octopuses and squid, boats, flags, fairies

AUTUMN

Leaves, jack-o'-lanterns, pumpkins, trees, spiderwebs, spiders, bats, skeleton

WINTER

Snow scene, reindeer, snowmen, snowflakes, stars, Christmas tree, elf

MELTED-CRAYON ROCKS

"Paint" small rocks with crayons. The crayons melt as they touch the hot rocks, creating vibrant small-scale artworks. Choose colors or draw themes related to the seasons.

MATERIALS

Small, smooth rocks
Baking sheet
Oven
Towel or mat to protect your table
Aluminum foil
Crayons (to protect fingers, do not use short stubs)
Oven mitt or mitten (optional)

INSTRUCTIONS

1. Wash and dry your rocks. Place them on the baking sheet and heat them in a 350°F oven for 10–15 minutes.
2. Protect your work surface with a place mat or towel covered with a sheet of foil.
3. Adult job: move one or two hot rocks at a time to the protected work surface. Make sure your child understands that the rocks are hot and that the child needs to be careful not to touch them with his or her fingers. (Put an oven mitt or winter mitten on their nondominant hand if desired.)
4. Press the tip of a crayon to a hot rock and watch as the crayon melts. Move the crayon around the rock slowly, letting the crayon melt as you work. Experiment with different colors and designs.
5. Let the rocks cool. Use the melted-crayon rocks for decoration or for pretend play.

IDEAS FOR PLAYING WITH MELTED-CRAYON ROCKS

Form letters, numbers, and designs.
Use as pretend food (great for cookies and candies) in a play kitchen or store.
Decorate sandbox cakes and mud pies (see page 160).
Use as special hopscotch markers (see page 134).
Use in counting and number games.
Use as part of other arts or crafts projects.

SPRING

Every spring is the only spring—
a perpetual astonishment.
—ELLIS PETERS

SPRING PROJECTS

CELEBRATING SPRING

SPRING IS BY FAR my favorite season. While I love aspects of each season and feel blessed to live in a climate that has all four, spring is the one I identify with and enjoy the most. Spring heralds the return of the sun's warmth, the renewal of life (nature's new year), and the reappearance of green and color everywhere. There's more time spent outdoors enjoying the first flowers and fresh smells, with birdsong as soundtrack, seedlings reaching for the sun, and baby animals cavorting.

Easter is the big holiday of the season, combining the magical (the Easter bunny, the Resurrection) with egg decorating, bunny crafts, and sweet treats, all decked out in pastel colors and now with warmer weather in which to enjoy them.

Easter Crafts

Much of our spring crafting energy goes toward dyeing eggs, decorating for Easter, and thinking of different ways to celebrate in an artful way. As a family, we experiment with different methods of dyeing and decorating eggs. We try our hands at creating baskets and growing our own Easter grass. With some Greek blood in the family, we also make a spectacular Greek Easter bread (leftovers make the best French toast!) with a dyed egg baked on top. We draw bunnies galore and even try out being bunnies ourselves. (Homemade rabbit ears help with that.)

EASTER EGG SUNCATCHERS

Create suncatchers in the shape of Easter eggs from colorful tissue paper, ribbon, lace, and contact paper. You can also use this method to create flowers, bunnies, or any spring or Easter-themed image.

MATERIALS

Scissors

Transparent contact paper (also called sticky-back plastic)

Tape

Marker

Ribbon and lace (optional)

Washi tape (optional)

Colored tissue paper

Colored masking or printed tape (optional)

Hole punch (optional)

INSTRUCTIONS

1. Cut the contact paper to the size desired (we aim for approximately 8" x 10"). Tape the contact paper to the table, paper side up. Carefully pull off the paper backing.

2. Use the marker to draw an oval egg

shape (on the sticky surface is fine), aiming to fill a large portion of the contact paper.

3. If you're using ribbon and lace, cut sections to span the width of the egg. Then press them to the sticky contact paper, creating stripes. Washi tape may be used this way as well.

4. Fill in the remaining areas with colored tissue paper that's been torn into pieces. Press them on flat or roll them into balls first.

5. Cut another sheet of contact paper the same size as the first, pull off the paper backing, and press this second sheet of contact paper on top of the one you decorated, sandwiching the Easter egg design between the two sheets. Cut out the Easter egg, preferably leaving about ½" beyond the marker line. An optional border can be added around the egg with masking tape.

6. Tape the suncatcher to a sunny window or punch a couple of holes in it and hang it with ribbon.

ARTFUL BUNNY EARS

Do-it-yourself bunny ears for Easter and pretend play become extra colorful with the addition of crayon-resist painting.

MATERIALS

Scissors
Bunny ears template (see page 326 or draw your own)
Heavy watercolor paper or card stock, 12" x 18"
Pencil or marker
Oil pastels or crayons (light colors work great for crayon resist)
Paintbrush
Watercolor paints (liquid watercolors are especially nice, but any will work)
Stapler

INSTRUCTIONS

1. Cut out the bunny ears from the printed template. Place them on the watercolor paper and trace the ears with pencil. Extend the headband lines across the width of the sheet. Alternatively, draw your bunny ears freehand directly on the heavy paper, with the headband along the long side. (Don't cut them out yet.)

2. Draw on the ears and headband with light-colored oil pastels or crayons. Paint over your drawing with watercolors. Let the painted bunny ears dry. (If the paper has buckled during the drying process, press it under heavy books overnight.)

3. Cut out the bunny ears, then staple the headband into a loop to fit over the head. (Be sure to test the fit before stapling.)

MAKING EASTER EGGS

There are two basic ways to prepare eggs for making Easter eggs: by blowing out eggs or making hard-boiled eggs. For eggs to hang on an Easter egg tree (page 72)— or just eggs that you can keep year after year—you'll want blown-out eggs. Hard-boiled eggs will need to be refrigerated after being decorated if you plan to eat them or thrown out after their time on display is over.

MATERIALS

For Blowing Eggs

Eggs, raw
Small nail or pin
Bowl
Water
Distilled white vinegar

For Hard-Boiled Eggs

Eggs, raw
Large pot
Water

INSTRUCTIONS

1. To blow out eggs, gently poke holes in each end of an egg using a small nail or pin. Make a smaller hole on the top and a slightly larger hole on the bottom. Poke the pin back in and, if possible, break the yolk.
2. Holding the egg over a bowl, press your lips over the smaller hole and blow (hard!) to expel the contents out the other hole. Continue with as many eggs as desired.
3. Wash the hollow eggs in warm water mixed with a generous splash of vinegar. Let them dry thoroughly before you decorate them.
4. To make hard-boiled eggs, place the

eggs in a large pot of cold water. Bring the water to a boil. Cover the pan and turn off the burner. Set a timer and let the eggs sit for 15 minutes.

DYE EASTER EGGS WITH FOOD COLORING

There is no need to buy a commercial egg dyeing kit. You can get equally vivid results with materials in your kitchen cabinet. You can combine this egg dyeing technique with many of the other Easter egg decorating ideas in this chapter.

MATERIALS

Water
Teakettle or pot
Cups, 1 for each color
Tablespoon
Food coloring or liquid watercolors
Distilled white vinegar
Spoons, 1 for each color
White eggs, hard-boiled or blown (page 52)
Egg carton(s) or drying rack

INSTRUCTIONS

1. Bring the water to a boil. Pour it into the cups, making sure to include enough water to cover an egg.
2. Add the food coloring (several drops) or liquid watercolors (1–2 tablespoons) and 1–2 tablespoons of vinegar to each cup and mix.
3. Use the spoons to gently lower an egg into each cup (you can leave the spoons there). Lift the eggs periodically to see if they have reached the colors desired. Leave the eggs in the dye briefly for lighter colors and longer for darker colors.
4. Remove the eggs from the dye and let them dry in your egg carton or on a drying rack.

MELTED-CRAYON EASTER EGGS

The melted-crayon procedure is hands-down our favorite Easter egg technique, both for the process and for the finished product. While we love experimenting with other ways to decorate eggs, we always do a big batch of melted-crayon Easter eggs.

MATERIALS

White eggs
Large pot
Water
Tongs
Egg carton(s) or egg cup
Crayons, all colors, but white and light colors are especially nice for the resist effect
Food coloring and distilled white vinegar or a commercial dye kit

INSTRUCTIONS

1. Boil the eggs in a large pot of water following the instructions on page 52. Gather your materials and prepare your work space. Be prepared to work as soon as the eggs are ready.

3. Use the tongs to transfer a hot egg to your egg carton or egg cup. Draw on the egg with crayons, letting the crayon melt as you draw.

4. Continue with the rest of the eggs, drawing on them one at a time and leaving the remainder in the hot water. (Alternatively, you can keep the eggs warm in a 250°F oven.)

5. Once your child has drawn on all the eggs, dye them using the food coloring technique on page 54 or with a commercial kit.

STAINED GLASS EASTER EGGS

The combination of marker drawings with a shiny, translucent glue and paint mixture gives these eggs an attractive stained glass effect.

MATERIALS

White eggs, blown or hard-boiled (page 52)
Sharpies or other permanent markers
White glue, such as Elmer's
Small cups
Tempera paint in an assortment of colors
Paintbrushes

INSTRUCTIONS

1. Draw pictures or designs on the white eggs with a Sharpie. Any color is fine, but a black marker will give a more realistic stained glass effect.
2. Squeeze a small amount of glue into each cup. Add an equal amount of paint, one color per cup, and mix.
3. Paint some of the glue-paint mixture on the Easter eggs, filling in the spaces between marker lines with color (or just painting all over, as younger children, especially, will do). To prevent the egg from sticking to the surface on which you dry it, paint only half of the egg and let it dry before turning it over and painting the other half.

YARN-PRINTED EASTER EGGS

Roll your eggs around in a little "nest" of paint-soaked yarn for a basketful of unique Easter eggs. This is a great tactile activity for young children!

MATERIALS

Scissors
Yarn or string
Small bowls
Acrylic paint (diluted half and half with water) or BioColor paint (see note below)
White eggs, blown or hard-boiled (page 52)

INSTRUCTIONS

1. Cut pieces of yarn and then pile it up in each bowl to create little nests.
2. Add the watered-down acrylic paint or BioColor paint to the yarn. Use your hands to mix the yarn and paint together thoroughly until the yarn is soaked with paint. Wash your hands.
3. Roll the eggs around in the paint-soaked yarn, printing them with the yarn designs. Let them dry.

Note: Acrylic paint is permanent and will stain clothes (though it will wash off hands). BioColor paint stays on the eggs well, but the paint will rub off the eggs if you use water and a scrubbing action.

GLITTER EGGS

Paint with glue and then add glitter for Easter eggs that pop—not to mention that are superpopular with the kids.

MATERIALS

Fine paintbrush
White or dyed eggs, blown or hard-boiled (page 52)
White glue
Glitter

INSTRUCTIONS

1. Use the paintbrush to paint a simple design on the egg with glue (such as stripes, zigzags, dots, a bunny, hearts, and so on).

2. Sprinkle glitter over the glue.

3. Add another glue design and a different color of glitter if desired. Let the eggs dry.

Washi tape, or a similar colorful, printed paper tape, is a simple and fun way for kids or adults to decorate Easter eggs.

MATERIALS

Scissors
Washi tape or other printed paper tape
White or dyed eggs (page 54), blown or hard-boiled (page 52)

INSTRUCTIONS

Cut washi tape into geometric or other shapes, or tear it into pieces. Adhere the tape to the egg in patterns, to form images, or randomly, as desired.

HOLEY EASTER EGGS

Trying a sticker-resist technique with hole-reinforcement stickers yields a unique Easter egg.

MATERIALS

Hole-reinforcement stickers
White eggs, blown or hard-boiled (page 52)
Food coloring and distilled white vinegar or a commercial dye kit

INSTRUCTIONS

1. Press hole-reinforcement stickers and/or other stickers all over the eggs as desired, either in patterns or randomly. Press the edges down firmly using your thumbnail.

2. Dye your sticker-covered eggs according to the instructions on page 54 or use a commercial kit.
3. Let the eggs dry. Peel off the stickers.

STICKER-RESIST-AND-MARKER EGGS

Combine a sticker-resist technique with permanent markers for a creative effect.

MATERIALS

Small stickers (see note below)
White eggs, blown or hard-boiled (page 52)
Sharpies or other permanent markers
Food coloring and distilled white vinegar

INSTRUCTIONS

1. Adhere the stickers to the eggs as desired, pressing the edges down firmly using the edge of your thumbnail.
2. Now draw on the sticker-covered egg with Sharpies.
3. Dye the eggs according to the instructions on page 54 or use a commercial kit.
4. Let the eggs dry. Peel off the stickers.

Note: Small stickers such as dot and price stickers from the office supply store are great for eggs. Some stickers are more resistant to removal than others. You may need to scrape them off with your thumbnail. Foil star stickers work especially well here and are easy to remove.

BLEEDING-TISSUE-PAPER EGGS

Using bleeding tissue paper to dye eggs is a fun technique for toddlers on up.

MATERIALS

Bleeding tissue paper (sometimes called art tissue) in multiple colors
Scissors (optional)
Water
Distilled white vinegar
Small bowl
Paintbrush
White eggs, blown or hard-boiled (page 52)

INSTRUCTIONS

1. Tear the colored tissue paper into small pieces. (Alternatively, use scissors to cut the tissue paper into geometric or other shapes.)
2. Mix the water with an equal amount of vinegar in a small bowl. Paint an egg with the water-vinegar mix. Press a piece of the bleeding tissue paper to the egg. Brush more of the water mixture over the tissue-paper piece. Repeat with more bleeding tissue paper until the egg is covered as desired. Continue with the remaining eggs.
3. Let the tissue paper dry. Remove the tissue-paper pieces and admire the colors left on the eggs.

MIXED-MEDIA EGGS

The egg is your canvas. These Easter eggs combine decoupage (always popular with kids) with drawings for a unique result every time.

MATERIALS

Scissors
Printed tissue paper (usually sold with gift wrap rather than art supplies) and/or printed paper napkins
White glue, such as Elmer's, or Mod Podge
Water
Small dish
Paintbrush or foam brush
White or dyed eggs (page 54), blown or hard-boiled (page 52)
Permanent markers, such as Sharpies
Glitter or sequins (optional)

INSTRUCTIONS

1. Cut images out of the printed tissue paper and/or paper napkins.
2. Thin the glue with an equal amount of water in a small dish and mix thoroughly or use Mod Podge on its own.
3. Use a brush to paint the glue mixture on the egg. Work on a section at a time rather than the entire egg. Press colored tissue paper or napkin shapes and images on the glue-covered egg. Brush more of the glue mixture over the tissue paper. Repeat the entire process until the egg is decorated to your satisfaction. Let the glue dry.
4. Draw pictures and designs on the eggs with permanent markers. Add glue and then glitter or sequins to your mixed-media eggs, if desired, for some extra sparkle.

DIY PAPIER-MÂCHÉ EASTER BASKET

What should you do with all of your decorated Easter eggs? Make your own colorful Easter baskets to showcase them. Creating with papier-mâché is a favorite craft activity for kids and allows them to make many different kinds of three-dimensional objects, both decorative and functional.

MATERIALS

Medium bowl in the desired size and shape of your Easter basket

Plastic wrap (the cling kind works especially well)

Plastic place mat or tray (optional)

White glue

Water

Shallow bowl

Paintbrush

Texas snowflakes (large coffee filters used for art), regular-size white basket coffee filters, or white paper towels

Colored tissue paper, cut or torn into squares or pieces

Scissors

Card stock or heavy watercolor paper

Stapler

Balloon

Shredded paper or grass

INSTRUCTIONS

1. Turn the medium bowl upside down and cover it with plastic wrap, tucking the excess inside the bowl. Set the plastic-covered bowl on another sheet of plastic wrap or on a nonstick surface such as a plastic place mat or tray.

2. Mix the glue with water (about equal parts) in a shallow bowl to create your paste mixture.

3. Use your hands or a paintbrush to cover the outer surface of the plastic wrap-covered bowl with a layer of the paste mixture. Press

a Texas snowflake over the bowl, tucking the edges inside. Rub more paste over the top of the coffee filter just applied and add another Texas snowflake, again tucking the edges underneath. (If you're using smaller coffee filters or paper towels, you may need to use more than one for each layer.)

4. Rub or brush another layer of paste over the covered bowl. Press colored tissue-paper pieces all over the bowl, layering them as desired. Let the bowl dry completely (1–2 days).

5. Turn the bowl over and use scissors to cut along the edge, pulling off the excess that was tucked inside. Gently remove the papier-mâché "basket" from the bowl.

6. Cut a strip of card stock approximately 2" x 18" to use for the basket handle. Staple to each side of the basket with two or three staples per side.

7. Blow up a balloon to fit inside the basket and under the handle, to support the handle as you cover it with wet papier-mâché. (*Tip:* Hold the balloon partially inside the basket as you blow it up.)

8. Rub or brush the handle with the glue mixture. Press colored tissue-paper pieces along the handle. Let the handle dry completely.

9. Pop and remove the balloon. If desired, you can add more colored-tissue-paper pieces to the interior of the basket and along the basket edge.

10. Fill the basket with shredded paper or real grass. (My daughters love to go outside with scissors and "trim" the lawn, gathering grass for their baskets.) Add Easter eggs.

TISSUE-PAPER NESTS

Scrunching up colored tissue paper, dipping it in a glue mixture, then sticking it to your bowl form is a simple and effective way to craft a nest.

MATERIALS

Small bowl
Plastic wrap
Plastic place mat or tray (optional)
White glue, such as Elmer's
Water
Bowl for glue
Colored tissue paper (facial tissue works as well)

INSTRUCTIONS

1. Turn the bowl upside down and cover it with plastic wrap, tucking the excess inside. Set the plastic-covered bowl on another sheet of plastic wrap or on a nonstick surface such as a plastic place mat or tray.
2. Mix the glue with water (about equal parts) in another bowl to create your paste mixture.
3. Tear off small- to medium-size pieces of colored tissue paper and scrunch them up into balls. Dip the end of each wad into the glue mixture and press it to the plastic-covered bowl. Repeat with tissue paper pieces until the bowl is entirely covered. Let the bowl dry, 1–2 days.
4. Gently pull the nest away from the bowl. Nestle a few Easter eggs inside and use it for your holiday decorating or for a spring nature table.

EASTER EGG TREE

Our Easter egg tree was inspired by one in my much-loved childhood copy of the book *A Time to Keep: The Tasha Tudor Book of Holidays*.

MATERIALS

Bucket or pot
Pebbles or sand
Large branch
Scissors
¼" wide ribbon
Hot glue gun
Blown and decorated Easter eggs (see pages 52 and 56–67)

INSTRUCTIONS

1. Fill the bucket partway with pebbles or sand. Stick the branch in the center of the bucket and hold it in place while you add more pebbles to stabilize your small tree.
2. Cut the ribbon into 5" lengths. Working with one piece at a time, fold the ribbon in half and use the hot glue gun to glue both ends to the top of an Easter egg, creating a hanging loop for the egg. Continue with the rest of your eggs.
3. Hang the eggs on your new Easter tree.

Spring Recipes

Spring is baby carrots, bountiful greens, fresh-picked peas, asparagus, rhubarb, and tiny strawberries with cream. It's the return of fresh, flavorful food to the more limited and heavy winter selection. Besides mixing salads with fresh greens and herbs and whipping up crepes, we try our hand at making birds' nests out of cookies or pretzel sticks.

BIRD'S NEST COOKIES

Bird's nest cookies are an adorable spring-themed treat that is superfun for kids to help make. This recipe is adapted from Ina Garten's Jam Thumbprint Cookies, substituting little candy eggs for the jam and making it a bit healthier with whole wheat flour and less sugar.

Makes 2 dozen

INGREDIENTS

1 cup (2 sticks) butter, at room temperature

½ cup sugar

1 teaspoon vanilla

2 cups white whole wheat flour

¼ teaspoon salt

1 egg

One bag sweetened, flaked coconut (about 7 oz.)

Small Easter egg candies or peanut M&M's (you can also use dried raisins and/or almonds for the eggs)

INSTRUCTIONS

1. Preheat the oven to 350°F. Line two cookie sheets with baking parchment.

2. Use an electric mixer to cream the butter and sugar in a large bowl. Add the vanilla. Add the flour and

salt and continue to mix until the dough forms.

3. Break off chunks of the cookie dough and, with your hands, roll them into medium-size balls (about 1½" in diameter).

4. In a small bowl, beat the egg with a tablespoon of water to use as an egg wash. Empty the bag of coconut flakes into a wide, shallow dish.

5. Dip the dough balls into the egg wash one by one, then transfer them to the dish of coconut and roll them around until they're thoroughly coated.

6. Place the cookies on a cookie sheet. Press your thumb gently but firmly into the center of each cookie, creating the nest shape. Bake for 25 minutes.

7. Press the Easter egg candies into the nest while the cookies are still warm. Eat warm or at room temperature.

STRAWBERRY SHORTCAKE MUFFINS

These muffins are a quick and easy alternative to traditional strawberry shortcake. Since they are low in sweetener, you can serve them for breakfast or a snack.

Makes 12 muffins

INGREDIENTS

For the Muffins

1 cup white whole wheat flour
1 cup all-purpose flour
½ cup sugar
½ teaspoon salt
½ cup (1 stick) butter, melted then cooled
2 large eggs
1 cup plain yogurt
1 teaspoon vanilla
1 cup diced strawberries

For the Filling

2 cups fresh strawberries
1–2 tablespoons sugar
1½ cups heavy whipping cream
1 teaspoon vanilla

INSTRUCTIONS

For the Muffins

1. Preheat the oven to 400°F and grease a 12-section muffin tin.
2. Whisk the dry ingredients together in a large bowl. Whisk the wet ingredients together in another bowl. Add wet mixture to dry mixture, stirring just enough to combine. Fold in strawberries.

3. Divide the muffin batter into muffin tin sections, sprinkle the tops with sugar if desired, and bake for 20 minutes.

To Assemble Your Strawberry Shortcakes

1. Slice the strawberries. Kids love to do this part. Even toddlers and preschoolers can cut strawberries with a butter knife. If desired, toss the strawberries with a sprinkle of the sugar before setting them aside.
2. Whip the heavy cream with an electric mixer until soft peaks form. Mix in 1 tablespoon or so of sugar and vanilla.
3. To assemble your shortcakes, slice the muffins in half horizontally, add a dollop of whipped cream to the bottom half and then a large spoonful of sliced strawberries. Set the top of the muffin over your goodies and enjoy.

GREEK EASTER BREAD

A tradition on my husband's side of the family, Greek Easter bread is a special once-a-year production that the kids love to help with. The dyed egg on top is traditionally red, but we don't always follow tradition. Harry, my husband, has adapted this *tsoureki* recipe slightly from the cookbook his father used regularly, *The Complete Greek Cookbook* by Theresa Karas Yianilos.

Makes 2 loaves

INGREDIENTS

½ teaspoon cinnamon
½ teaspoon anise seed
½ teaspoon finely chopped orange peel
1 bay leaf
½ cup water
2 packets active dry yeast (4½ teaspoons)
1⅛ cup milk
½ cup butter (1 stick)
7 cups all-purpose flour
1 cup + 1 tablespoon sugar
2 teaspoons vanilla
1 teaspoon salt
3 large eggs, beaten
Olive oil
Egg wash (1 egg yolk whisked with 1 tablespoon water)
¼ cup sesame seeds
1 more egg, hard-boiled and dyed dark red using food coloring (see pages 53, 54)

INSTRUCTIONS

1. In a small saucepan, mix the cinnamon, anise seed, orange peel, and bay leaf with the ½ cup water. Bring the water to a boil, then cover, turn off the burner, and allow the ingredients to steep and cool. When cooled, strain the liquid with a sieve or cheesecloth into a small bowl.

2. Heat the milk in a small saucepan until hot but not boiling, then turn off the burner. Add the butter and stir until melted.

3. Pour the milk-butter mixture into a large bowl and let cool to lukewarm. Whisk in yeast, 1 cup flour, and 1 tablespoon sugar. Cover and set aside for 30 minutes or until frothy.

4. Stir in the eggs, flavored water, vanilla, 1 cup sugar, and salt.

5. Add the remaining flour. Mix the batter with a wooden spoon, then turn it out onto a floured counter to knead for 10 minutes until smooth and elastic.

6. Form the dough into a ball and place it in an oiled bowl, turning the dough once so that the top is lightly oiled as well. Cover the bowl and set it in a warm spot until the dough has doubled, about 2 hours.

7. Punch the dough down and knead it lightly. Divide the dough into six equal pieces, rolling each into a long rope with your hands. Pinch the ends of three of the ropes together, then braid them. Tuck the ends under slightly and place the loaf on a parchment-covered baking sheet. Repeat with the other three ropes, placing the second loaf on a separate baking sheet. Let rise for 1 hour.

8. Brush the braided loaves with egg wash and sprinkle them with sesame seeds. Nestle the dyed eggs in the top of the braids.

9. Bake the loaves in a 350°F oven for 45 minutes.

10. Serve the bread warm or at room temperature. We usually use leftovers to make French toast the following day.

FRUITY SPRING PANCAKES

Create flowers, eggs in nests, and other shapes with pancake batter that's been tinted with fresh fruit. My daughters get very excited when they see each new pancake design hot off the griddle.

INGREDIENTS

½ cup blueberries (thaw first if frozen)
½ cup strawberries (thaw first if frozen)
2 cups white whole wheat flour
2 teaspoons baking powder
1 teaspoon baking soda
2 tablespoons sugar
2–3 large eggs
4 tablespoons butter, melted and cooled slightly
2 cups milk
Butter, syrup, and fresh fruit for toppings

INSTRUCTIONS

1. Puree the blueberries and strawberries separately in a blender, rinsing out the blender between berries. Set purees aside in separate bowls.

2. Mix the dry ingredients together in a large bowl. In a medium bowl, whisk together the eggs and melted butter.

3. Add ⅓ of the flour mixture and ⅓ of the egg mixture to each of the fruit purees and stir the batter until just combined. Combine the remaining ⅓ each of the flour and egg mixtures together with the milk—this is your plain batter. (*Note:* If any batter is too thick, add a little milk.) Put each pancake batter into a separate squeeze bottle or a sandwich bag (if you're using a plastic bag, cut a small hole in one corner).

4. Squeeze both the tinted and the plain batters onto a hot, greased

griddle in the shape of flowers, eggs, nests, birds, and other creations. Cook until the edges of the pancake are dry. Flip the pancake and cook it on the other side.

5. Serve with butter, syrup, and fresh fruit.

VARIATIONS

If desired, create additional colors with other pureed fruits or vegetables or with food coloring. Add a dash of sprinkles for speckled eggs.

CROCK-POT MILLET PORRIDGE

Have a hot, healthy breakfast ready when you wake up. Millet is a nutritious and delicious whole grain that makes a great breakfast porridge.

INGREDIENTS

1 cup millet
4 cups water
1 teaspoon vanilla
2 tablespoons butter
Toppings such as fresh or dried fruit, honey, shredded coconut, and/or nuts
Milk, kefir, or yogurt

INSTRUCTIONS

1. Mix the millet, water, vanilla, and butter in your Crock-Pot or slow cooker. Cook on low for 6–8 hours.

2. Serve the porridge with the desired toppings and milk, kefir, or yogurt.

RASPBERRY-LEMON CREAM CHEESE COFFEE CAKE

As good for an afternoon snack as it is for breakfast.

For the Coffee Cake

2¼ cups white whole wheat flour
¾ cup sugar
Zest from 2 lemons
¾ cup butter, cut into ½" pieces
½ cup ground or finely chopped almonds
1 teaspoon baking powder
½ teaspoon baking soda
¼ teaspoon salt
¾ cup plain yogurt
1 egg
1½ cups fresh or frozen raspberries

For the Filling

8 oz. softened cream cheese
¼ cup sugar
1 egg
Juice of 1 lemon

INSTRUCTIONS

1. Preheat the oven to 350°F. Grease and flour a 10" springform pan.
2. Mix the flour, sugar, and lemon zest in a food processor. Add the butter to the flour. Pulse the butter-flour mixture until it is crumbly.
3. Reserve 1 cup of the butter/flour crumbs for topping. Add the ground almonds to the reserved crumbs.
4. Place the remaining crumbs in a large bowl and add the baking

powder, baking soda, salt, yogurt, and egg. Mix the batter until it's mostly smooth. Gently stir in the raspberries. Use a spatula or your hands to spread the batter over the bottom of the springform pan.

5. To make the filling, process the softened cream cheese, sugar, 1 egg, and lemon juice in a food processor until smooth. Pour the filling over the batter in the pan. Sprinkle the reserved crumbs on top.

6. Bake for 1 hour. Test for doneness by inserting a toothpick in the center of the cake. If it comes out clean, the cake is done. Let it cool completely.

BIRD'S NEST SNACK

Build this edible bird's nest out of a delicious peanut butter dough and pretzel sticks. Add candy eggs or a little marshmallow Peep once the nest is completed.

Makes 4 nests

INGREDIENTS

1 cup peanut butter or other nut butter
½ cup powdered sugar
2 tablespoons cocoa powder
1 cup powdered milk
¼ cup honey
Pretzel sticks
Candy eggs or marshmallows

INSTRUCTIONS

1. In a medium bowl, mix the peanut butter, powdered sugar, cocoa powder, honey, and powdered milk together with an electric mixer.
2. Divide the dough into four and give each child a dough section and some pretzels.
3. Create a "pinch pot" with the dough by first forming it into a ball, then putting your thumb in the center and working around the perimeter with your thumb and fingers. Widen the central indentation until you are satisfied with the nest.
4. Poke and place pretzel sticks and pretzel pieces in the peanut butter dough to create a more realistic nest. Note that younger children may just poke the pretzels into the dough ball for a more abstract sculpture effect.
5. Add a few marshmallows or candy eggs to the nest to serve as eggs. Or include a marshmallow Peep for a bird.
6. Once the nest is complete, admire it and then eat it.

CREPES TWO WAYS

Crepes are a favorite with kids and adults alike. Fill them with spring vegetables for a savory dish or with fruit for a sweet one.

INGREDIENTS

3 large eggs
1 cup milk
2 tablespoons butter, melted, plus more for the pan
1 cup white whole wheat flour
½ teaspoon salt

INSTRUCTIONS

1. Mix the eggs, milk, 2 tablespoons of butter, flour, and salt in a blender. Let the batter sit for 1 hour.
2. Pour ¼ cup of the batter onto a heated, nonstick pan. Tilt the pan in all directions to spread the batter thinly to about 6"–8" in diameter. Cook for 1–2 minutes before flipping the crepe and cooking it for 30–45 seconds on the reverse side. Remove the crepe from the pan and keep it warm in a 250°F oven. Repeat the process to cook more crepes.
3. Add your choice of savory or sweet toppings (see below) to your crepes and roll them up.

Fill with Spring Vegetables

Spring vegetables, such as spinach, peas, or baby carrots, lightly steamed or sautéed with butter
Chopped herbs, such as parsley or chives (optional)
Shredded cheese of choice (optional)

Fill with Fruit

Berries or fruit, chopped or mashed
Mascarpone or cottage cheese (optional)
Sweetener, such as a drizzle of honey or a teaspoon of sugar (optional)

SPRING GREENS SALAD

Salads are an easy way for kids to be involved in making dinner—and they're more likely to eat their vegetables if they're involved in growing and preparing them.

INGREDIENTS

Lettuce, spinach, arugula, mizuna, or other spring greens
Edible flowers, such as pansies or chive blossoms (optional)
Fresh herbs, such as parsley, cilantro, basil, or chives (optional)
Spring vegetables, such as peas, radishes, and baby carrots
Olive oil
Vinegar, such as balsamic or the Herbal Vinegar on page 90
Salt and pepper

INSTRUCTIONS

1. Wash and dry the greens. Place them in a salad bowl. Add the edible flowers, herbs, and vegetables as desired. Toss the salad.

2. Drizzle the greens with olive oil and vinegar and toss again. Season with salt and pepper. Serve.

HERBAL VINEGAR

It's so easy and satisfying to make your own herb-infused vinegar to use in salad dressings and cooking.

INGREDIENTS

Fresh herbs, such as basil or chive blossoms
White balsamic vinegar

INSTRUCTIONS

1. Wash and dry your herbs and roughly chop them. If you're using chive blossoms, leave the blossoms intact.
2. Loosely pack jelly jars or other small glass jars (with lids) with the clean herbs. Pour the vinegar over the herbs, leaving a ½"–1" space at the top. Place a piece of parchment paper over the top, then screw the lid on.
3. Place the jars in a cool, dark place, such as a cupboard, for 1–2 weeks, or until the contents reach your desired flavor intensity.
4. Strain the herbal vinegar through a strainer or sieve to remove the herbs. Return the vinegar to the glass jars. Try it out on your next spring salad (page 88).

Spring Crafts

In spring our imagination is captured by the birds, their nesting and laying of eggs, and their chicks hatching. As a family of young learners, we do our best to observe, from a respectful distance, while helping when we can—by making birdhouses, filling the bird feeders, supplying nesting materials, and incorporating bird habitats into our garden. We treasure fragile robin's egg fragments we find beneath trees, try to re-create eggs and nests ourselves, and read thought-provoking children's picture books to learn as much as possible (books about birds are on page 335).

OUR FAVORITE BOOKS ABOUT SPRING

Waiting Out the Storm by JoAnn Early Macken
And Then It's Spring by Julie Fogliano
How Mama Brought the Spring by Fran Manushkin
A New Beginning: Celebrating the Spring Equinox by Wendy Pfeffer
Mud by Mary Lyn Ray

BLUEBIRD PAPER CHAIN

Bring birds indoors with this artful paper chain. Perfect for spring or party decor!

MATERIALS

Scissors
Watercolor paper or other heavy paper, 12" x 18"
Bird template (see page 327 or draw your own)
Paintbrush
Paint: tempera or BioColor
Glitter (optional)
Stapler
Tape

INSTRUCTIONS

1. Cut the paper into three strips, 18" x 4". Fold each strip into thirds, end to end, accordion style.
2. Hold the bird template over the accordion-folded paper and cut through all layers, making sure to leave at least ¼" of folded paper between the birds (at the beaks and tails).
3. Paint the paper birds. Add glitter if desired. Let the paint dry.
4. Connect two or more paper bird chains together with staples or tape. Hang the chains with tape to decorate your home.

VARIATIONS

Make paper chains with any spring-themed image. Ideas include flowers (my daughter makes a lot of these), bunnies, eggs, lambs, and chicks.

LEAFY MASTERPIECE

Make botanical art worth hanging by printing with leaves and flowers on canvas.

MATERIALS

Newspapers or splat mat
Paintbrush
Stretched canvas, any size
Acrylic or BioColor paint
Leaves and ferns
Water-based printing ink (acrylic paint works too)
Large plate or acrylic box frame, for rolling out the ink (see page 349)
Mini paint roller (from the hardware store, used for corners and trim in house
 painting)
Newspaper and scrap paper
Brayer (hard rubber roller, found at arts and crafts supply stores) or old rolling pin
Plain white or light-colored paper
Scissors
Mod Podge or glue

INSTRUCTIONS

1. Protect your work surface with newspapers or a splat mat.
2. Paint the front and sides of your plain canvas with acrylic paint or BioColor (a light color works best). Use all one color or a combination of colors. If you want a white surface, paint it white rather than leaving the canvas uncoated. Let the paint dry.
3. Go on a nature walk around your yard or neighborhood to collect leaves of various sizes and shapes. You can include leaves from houseplants as well.
4. Prepare for leaf printing by gathering all of your materials.
5. Squeeze a small amount of ink on the plate. Roll it around with the paint roller to coat the roller thinly.
6. Place a leaf, vein side up, on a sheet

of newspaper or scrap paper. Roll the paint roller over the leaf to coat it evenly.

7. Set the leaf, paint side down, on the canvas you have prepared for the print. Place a clean piece of scrap paper over the leaf. Press down firmly with your hands or roll a clean brayer over the paper-covered leaf to press it down evenly. Carefully lift up the paper and leaf to reveal your print.

8. Continue to print leaves and ferns in one or more colors on the canvas until you are happy with your design. Make some leaf prints on paper as well. Let the prints dry.

9. Cut out the paper leaf prints and, using Mod Podge or glue, glue them to your canvas as desired for a more complex and layered botanical image. Let the prints dry, then hang them.

VARIATIONS

You can also use this method to decorate paper, including stationery (see page 98), wrapping paper, and journals, and to make your own stickers (see page 96). For leaf printing on fabric, see the activity on page 100.

LEAF STICKERS

Print your own seasonal stickers with new spring leaves. Use for art or gifts or to decorate letters and cards.

MATERIALS

Newspapers or a splat mat

Small fresh leaves

Water-based printing ink or acrylic paint

Large plate or acrylic box frame, for rolling out the ink

Newspaper and scrap paper

Mini paint roller (from the hardware store, used for corners and trim in house painting)

Full sheet of sticker paper (sold as full-sheet address labels)

Brayer (hard rubber roller, found at arts and crafts supply stores) or rolling pin

Pen (optional)

Scissors

INSTRUCTIONS

1. Protect your work surface with newspapers or a splat mat.
2. Follow steps 3–7 for Leafy Masterpiece (see page 94), making your leaf prints on full-size sticker sheets instead of on canvas. Let the stickers dry.
3. Use a pen to outline the leaf prints if desired.
4. Cut out the stickers, leaving a ⅛"–¼" margin around the pen line.
5. Pull off the paper backing and apply the stickers where desired, such as on envelopes or blank note cards.

BOTANICAL STATIONERY

Decorate blank cards and envelopes with botanical prints. Great for Mother's Day.

MATERIALS

Newspapers or a splat mat

Leaves and ferns

Water-based printing ink (acrylic paint works too.)

Large plate or acrylic box frame, for rolling out the ink

Newspaper and scrap paper

Mini paint roller (from the hardware store, used for corners and trim in house painting)

Plain white or light-colored paper postcards, note cards, envelopes, or journals

Brayer (hard rubber roller, found at arts and crafts supply stores) or old rolling pin

INSTRUCTIONS

1. Protect your work surface with newspapers or a splat mat.
2. Follow steps 3–7 for Leafy Masterpiece (see page 94), making your leaf prints on note cards, postcards, and envelopes instead of on canvas. Let the prints dry.
3. Add a greeting or note and drop them in the mail. Or tie a set of cards together with a ribbon and present them as a gift with some homemade leaf stickers (page 96).

PRINT YOUR OWN SPRING FABRIC

Decorate your own fabric with gorgeous prints of all the new spring leaves and ferns.

MATERIALS

Newspaper or a splat mat

Spoon

Fabric paint (I like Jacquard brand.)

Large plate or acrylic box frame, for rolling out the ink

Mini paint roller (from the hardware store, used for corners and trim in house painting)

Leaves and ferns

Newspaper and scrap paper

Plain white or light-colored cotton fabric (or white T-shirt, scarf, skirt, handkerchief, pillowcase, napkins, and so forth)

Brayer (hard rubber roller, found at arts and crafts supply stores) or old rolling pin

Iron

Ironing board

INSTRUCTIONS

1. Prepare for leaf printing by protecting your work surface with newspaper or a splat mat. Gather all of your materials.

2. Put a couple spoonfuls of fabric paint on the plate. Roll it around with the paint roller to coat the roller thinly.

3. Place a leaf, vein side up, on a sheet of newspaper or scrap paper. Roll the paint roller over the leaf to coat it evenly.

4. Set the leaf, paint side down, on the fabric where you want the print. Set a clean piece of paper over the leaf. Roll the brayer over the paper-covered leaf to press it down evenly. Carefully lift up the paper and leaf to reveal your print.

5. Continue to print leaves and ferns

in one or more colors until you are happy with your fabric design.

6. Let the paint dry overnight, and then iron, following the instructions on the fabric paint bottle to set the paint. Once the fabric paint is "set," you can wash and dry it as you would any fabric.

7. Use your new fabric to create a pillow, skirt, napkins, or flag. Or, if you printed directly on a clothing item, it's ready to wear and enjoy!

MARSHMALLOW SCULPTURES

Pastel-colored marshmallows give a little spring twist to this childhood favorite. Perfect for rainy spring days that keep the family indoors.

MATERIALS

Marshmallows, pastel-colored or white (see note)
Toothpicks, round style is best

INSTRUCTIONS

Build structures with the marshmallows by connecting them with toothpicks. Continue to add toothpicks and marshmallows until satisfied with your sculpture.

Note: It can be easier to work with stale marshmallows. Spread the marshmallows on a cookie sheet and leave them out for a week or two to make them firmer.

FOREST DIORAMA

Learn about forest ecosystems and celebrate Earth Day or Arbor Day by creating your own tabletop forest.

MATERIALS

Branches, leaves, and flowers
Playdough (see page 16) or clay
Fabric or other additions, as desired
Drawing tools
Paper
Animal figurines (optional), drawings, or pictures

INSTRUCTIONS

1. First, go on a nature walk around your yard or local park, collecting branch tips, leaves, and flowers. (*Note:* Some public areas have rules against picking vegetation.)
2. Back home, create miniature trees and shrubs by sticking your nature items into balls of playdough so that they stand upright.
3. Arrange the trees and shrubs into a forest on a tabletop. (Preferably not the dining table, so the forest doesn't have to be removed at dinnertime.)
4. Add additional features of the natural ecosystem such as a river or lake (perhaps a blue scarf or play silk), mountains, rocks, and a sun. Use playdough, fabric, magazine pictures, drawings on paper, or your own ideas to add to your landscape.
5. Now populate your new forest with animals, birds, and insects, using play figurines if desired and/or paper animals that are drawn (or found in magazines) and cut out.
6. Play with your new forest diorama and use it as a discussion starting point about local or world ecosystems.

The Family Garden

I love spring anywhere, but if I could choose
I would always greet it in a garden.
—RUTH STOUT

Gardening with children is a way to connect them with the magic of the natural world (an unassuming seed springs to life with the addition of warmth and water), and it will help them gain a greater understanding and appreciation of where our food comes from.

Even if you don't consider yourself a gardener, I recommend giving it a try, side by side with your kids. Planting seeds and seedlings, watering them, and watching them grow day by day is rewarding for gardeners of any age. Gardening is mostly easy, even for the novice. Fill a small garden or containers with kid-friendly flowers and vegetables such as peas, carrots, zinnias, and pumpkins and give them plenty of water and sunshine, following instructions on the seed packets.

A garden is like a miniature world where children can observe, up close and personal, and more regularly, some of the natural cycles of life. (Rumor has it that fairies live there too.)

OUR FAVORITE BOOKS ABOUT GARDENING

Roots, Shoots, Buckets, and Boots by Sharon Lovejoy
The Garden Classroom: Hands-on Activities in Math, Science, Literacy, and Art by Cathy James
A Seed Is Sleepy by Diana Hutts Aston
Flower Garden by Eve Bunting
Planting a Rainbow by Lois Ehlert
Isabella's Garden by Glenda Millard

GARDEN WISH FLAGS

Our wish flags flutter in the breeze, carrying our hopes and dreams for the garden and the season.

MATERIALS

Paper or cardboard
White cotton fabric
Light-colored chalk
Pinking shears or regular fabric scissors
Tape, painter's or masking
Pentel brand fabric crayons
Iron
Ironing board
Colorful fabric for backing (optional)
Sewing machine
¼"–½" wide ribbon

INSTRUCTIONS

1. Use the paper to create a triangle template in the size of your choosing. Trace the triangle onto the white fabric with chalk. Cut it out using the pinking shears (an adult job).

2. Tape the fabric triangles to your work surface with the painter's tape, pulling the fabric taut while you tape it down.

3. Draw your garden wishes on the white fabric using the fabric crayons. Our wish flags often include sun, rain, butterflies, birds, bees for pollination, worms, and lots of flowers.

4. Remove the painter's tape.

5. Iron the fabric to set the designs, following the instructions on the fabric crayons.

6. If you'd like to back each triangle with a brightly colored fabric, do so now. Sew the ribbon along the top of the wish flags, connecting them to form a banner.

7. Hang the wish flags in your garden where they can work their magic.

BEADED GARDEN ORNAMENTS

Decorate your garden with colorful beaded garden ornaments. Stringing beads is fun for children of all ages and especially great for honing fine motor skills in younger ones.

MATERIALS

Pipe cleaners
Small wooden dowels
Assortment of colorful beads
Hot glue gun
Thin, flexible wire (such as jewelry wire)

INSTRUCTIONS

1. Wrap and twist one end of a pipe cleaner around one end of a dowel. String beads onto the other end of the pipe cleaner and then twist the end of the pipe cleaner down, to hold the beads on. Add another pipe cleaner to the dowel and continue the process until you have five or six beaded pipe cleaners on your dowel.

2. Squeeze glue from the hot glue gun over the pipe cleaner ends that are wrapped around the top of the dowel (to secure them all in place). If desired, glue a large bead at the very top of the dowel.

3. Make as many beaded garden ornaments as desired and then wire them to stakes or poles in your garden. We use ours at the top of the poles that hold up our garden wish flags.

PAINTED BIRDHOUSES

Colorful birdhouses brighten up the garden, add an inviting nesting spot for neighborhood birds, and are lots of fun to paint.

MATERIALS

Paintbrushes
Plain wood birdhouse (from craft or garden stores or your local bird club)
Liquid watercolor paints
Foam brush
Acrylic sealer or outdoor Mod Podge
Mounting hardware

INSTRUCTIONS

1. Paint your birdhouse with one or more colors of liquid watercolor paint. Let the paint dry thoroughly. Keep the bird perch, the entry hole, and the interior free of all paints and sealers. Birds, especially fledglings, need the rougher, more natural wood to climb in and out.
2. Use the foam brush to paint one or two coats of acrylic sealer over the outside of the birdhouses. Let the sealer dry.
3. Mount your colorful new birdhouses as desired on poles, fences, or other safe places. (Keep them high enough that cats and other animals can't reach the nests.)

VARIATION

Instead of painting the birdhouses, consider decorating them with leaves, lichens, sticks, mosses, and bark for a more natural bird abode. Attach the nature items with wire or thumbtacks (pressed in firmly so birds can't remove them when borrowing house decorations for nest making).

GARDEN LOOM

A simple wood frame can be built to use for garden weaving with a combination of nature materials, fabrics, and ribbons.

Handsaw

1" x 1.5" wood strips, 24' total in length (4 pieces at 48" for the loom, 2 pieces at 24" for the ground posts, plus extra for braces)

Electric drill and screwdriver

Exterior coated wood screws, $1\frac{7}{8}$" long

Small shovel

Concrete (optional)

Twine or yarn

Natural materials such as grasses, flowers, and twigs

Assorted fabric strips, ribbons, yarns

INSTRUCTIONS

1. Use the handsaw to cut four lengths of wood into 48" strips. Cut two lengths of wood into 24" strips.

2. To form the loom, make an open square out of three of the 48" wood lengths, placing the fourth 8" up the two side strips. Drill pilot holes on each corner and attach the wood strips to each other with screws.

3. Attach the ground posts to the square using four screws on each side and leaving 12"–16" for extending underground.

4. Dig two holes with a small shovel or trowel, about 4' apart (line them up with the loom posts as you're measuring and digging).

5. Stick the two garden loom legs into the holes and tamp them down firmly with soil. (Alternatively, you can pour in a small amount of concrete to make the loom sturdier.)

6. Brace the bottom of the loom with extra wood extending at a 45-degree angle from the legs toward the center of the bottom of the square.

HOW TO WEAVE ON THE GARDEN LOOM

1. Tie the twine to the loom, either in the traditional vertical warp pattern or in a more free-form spiderweb design, as pictured here.

2. Weave flowers, grasses, and twigs through the twine as well as fabric strips, yarn, and ribbons. (Don't be surprised if you see birds snagging a few items to line their nests.)

Note: If you used all-natural materials such as cotton and wool in your weaving, you can cut it all off and toss the whole thing in the compost when you're ready to make a new weaving.

VARIATION

Use a hula hoop instead of building a frame for your loom. Lean it against a tree or hang it from a branch. The round shape is best suited to a spiderweb-type weaving.

WEAVE A BEANPOLE TEEPEE

We grow beans up a simple teepee frame almost every year. The teepee itself is fun for children to help erect, and the beans sprout and grow quickly, covering the frame with delicious fresh vegetables and forming a living, child-size fort.

MATERIALS

Shovel
6–8 bamboo or other poles, 8'–10' long
Garden twine
Assorted fabric strips, ribbons, yarns
Natural materials such as grasses, flowers, and twigs
Pole bean seeds, soaked overnight

INSTRUCTIONS

1. Prepare the ground for your beanpole teepee in an area that gets 6–8 hours of sun a day. If you're building this on the lawn, dig up the turf in a horseshoe shape about 6'–8' in diameter (leaving space for a door) and amend the soil with compost.

2. Create the teepee frame with the bamboo poles evenly spaced, securing the bottom ends of the poles in the soil about 6" deep and tying the top ends together with twine.

3. Tie and wrap twine between the teepee poles from top to bottom, leaving a space open between two poles for the doorway. Tie on and weave in ribbons, fabrics, flowers, and the like.

4. Plant bean seeds around the base of the teepee and water thoroughly. *Note:* You can build your teepee anytime during the spring, but bean planting time varies according to your climate, so make sure to read the seed packet for guidance.

5. The beans will grow up the structure, creating a living teepee playhouse.

CONCRETE STEPPING-STONES

Artful stepping-stones can be created by pressing pebbles, shells, leaves, and treasures (marbles, sea glass, little toy figurines) into wet concrete.

MATERIALS

12" plastic flowerpot saucers (the inexpensive transparent kind)
Petroleum jelly
Plastic drop cloth or newspaper
1 bag of Quikrete
Disposable plastic gloves
Pebbles, shells, leaves, and other nature items

INSTRUCTIONS

1. Grease the inside of the plastic pot saucers with the petroleum jelly. Arrange them on the plastic drop cloth.
2. Adult job only: Mix the concrete according to the instructions on the bag. Use the gloves and refrain from breathing the concrete dust. Pour the concrete into the prepared molds and smooth the top.
3. Press pebbles and other nature items into the surface of the concrete in any design desired.
4. Let the stepping-stones dry for 2 days, then remove them from the molds. Place them in the garden.

SUMMER

———

In June, as many as a dozen species may
burst their buds on a single day. No man
can heed all of these anniversaries; no man
can ignore all of them.

—ALDO LEOPOLD

SUMMER PROJECTS

CELEBRATING SUMMER

IN SUMMER BOTH NATURE and children are bustling with energy. The birds belt out the songs, the insects buzz, the gardens burst (with a dizzying riot of color and scent), and the kids have never been so busy. We respond both by slowing down (all the better to enjoy it) and speeding up. The long, light-filled hours and warm weather inspire us to be active and do more.

Vegetable gardens; farmers' markets; fresh salads with crunchy cucumbers, just-picked tomatoes, and flavorful basil capture the essence of summer for me—accented by the chatter of exuberant children.

And it isn't summer without water to cool us off. We run through the sprinkler, take trips to the beach, frequent swimming holes, and dance in warm afternoon rainstorms.

I think I speak for more than just myself when I say we all feel a bit healthier in the summer than at other times of the year. Being active, getting fresh air and sunlight, taking more time to relax and play, and eating fresh from the garden and orchard can't help but make us our best selves.

Summer Crafts

In summer the greater emphasis on outdoor living and exploring means that the crafts of the season are often created outside or created with the intention of being used outside. We make artful pinwheels to twirl in the wind and beaded bubble wands for that old favorite, bubble blowing. And we try our hands at sand-casting, both at the beach and in the sandbox.

ARTFUL PINWHEELS

Create colorful pinwheels from watercolor-resist paintings.

MATERIALS

Poster board, watercolor paper, or card stock
Crayons
Paintbrush
Watercolor paint (we used liquid watercolors)
Scissors
Ruler
Pencil
Artwork remnants or colored construction paper
Pushpin
Small wooden dowels (from the craft store) or pencils
Straight pins (the kind with a little ball head)
Small round beads with holes through the center
Hot glue gun

1. Draw on the poster board with crayons, pressing hard. White and light colors work especially well for this technique, called watercolor resist. Paint over the entire paper with watercolors. Let the paint dry.

2. Turn the poster board over and paint the reverse side with a contrasting color of watercolor paint. Let it dry again.

3. Cut the watercolor-resist artwork into 6" squares (smaller or larger work as well, but this is a good size to start with). Turn a square over and use a ruler and a pencil to draw straight lines from corner to corner, crossing in the center. Use scissors to cut along the drawn lines, stopping 1"–2" from the center.

4. Cut 1"–2" circles out of artwork remnants or colored construction paper.

5. Create holes in preparation for assembly: Poke a pushpin into the side of the dowel, near the top. Remove the pin, leaving a hole. Use the same pin to poke holes in the center of the penciled X as well as in the pointed end of each spoke. Also poke a hole in the center of the circles.

6. To assemble, insert a straight pin through the hole in the center of one of the circles, then through each of the four spokes, one at a time, and then finally through the center of the penciled X. Slip a bead onto the end of the pin (so there will be a bead between the dowel and the pinwheel), then add a dab from the hot glue gun to the sharp end of the pin. Poke the glue-covered pin end into the hole in the dowel. The hot glue dries quickly.

7. Blow your pinwheel to make it spin, or hold it up to the wind.

PICNIC NAPKINS

Double-sided napkins in summery fabrics are perfect to take along on a picnic. This is an easy sewing project for adults or kids and an especially good one for those just beginning to use a sewing machine. In the latter case, don't fret about mistakes or seams that are not straight—my daughter went off the bias tape a few times, and I just helped her back up a bit and get on track again.

MATERIALS

1 yard each of 2 lightweight printed cotton fabrics
Bias tape, extra-wide double-fold, in a coordinating color
Pins
Sewing machine
Thread to match the bias tape

INSTRUCTIONS

1. Line up the two fabrics, wrong sides together, and cut squares through both layers in the size desired. Ours are about 12" square.
2. With the squares of fabric still layered together, attach the bias tape with pins, starting at one corner and sandwiching the edges of the napkin between the two sides of the bias tape.
3. Sew along the inner edge of the narrow side of the bias tape, removing pins as you go.
4. Repeat with the rest of the napkins.

FLOWER CROWNS

Make stunning flower crowns to celebrate the floral bounty of summer. These are great for pretend-play accessories or as a unique party activity.

Crown template (see page 328)
Pencil
Poster board or card stock
Scissors
X-Acto knife
Cutting mat or cardboard
Transparent contact paper (also called sticky-back plastic)
Flowers
Tape

INSTRUCTIONS

1. Using the crown template, trace the crown shape on the poster board, including the large inset sections where the flower jewels will go.

2. Cut out the crown. Scissors work best for the outside of the crown, and an X-Acto knife will work best for cutting out the insets. X-Acto knives are for adults only. Make sure to protect your work surface with a cutting mat or cardboard if using an X-Acto knife.

3. Pull the paper backing off a piece of contact paper and lay it on the table, sticky side up. Press the crown to the contact paper, then cut away the excess contact paper from the outer edges, leaving the contact paper exposed in the inset sections.

4. Press flower petals to the contact paper, creating a bejeweled, stained glass effect.

5. Cut small pieces of contact paper slightly larger than the inset sections of the crown and press these over the flower-petal stained glass.

6. Wrap the crown around your head and tape it in place.

The same technique used for the flower stained glass crowns can also be used to create necklaces.

MATERIALS

Card stock
Scissors
X-Acto knife
Cutting mat or cardboard
Transparent contact paper (also called sticky back-plastic)
Flowers
Hole punch
Yarn

INSTRUCTIONS

1. Cut "doughnuts" out of card stock about 3"–4" in diameter. Scissors work best for the outside of the circle, and an X-Acto knife will work best for cutting out the inset circle. X-Acto knives are for adults only. Make sure to protect your work surface with a cutting mat or cardboard if using an X-Acto knife.

2. Cut circles out of the contact paper, slightly larger than the hole. Pull off the paper backing and stick it over the hole, so that it overlaps the edges by a bit.

3. Press flower petals to the sticky contact paper. Cover the flower design with a second circle of contact paper.

4. Punch a hole at the top of the circle. Thread a length of yarn through the hole and tie the ends together to create the necklace.

MELTED-CRAYON STAINED GLASS BUNTING

Hang this melted-crayon stained glass bunting where the summer sun can shine through it.

Cheese grater
Crayons
Bowls or muffin tin
Iron
Wax paper
Ironing board
Newsprint or scrap paper
Scissors
Sewing machine or hot glue gun (see note below)

INSTRUCTIONS

1. Follow steps 1–6 of the Melted-Crayon Suncatchers on page 23.
2. Cut the melted-crayon stained glass into triangles, either freehand or with a paper template if you prefer a uniform size.
3. Use a sewing machine to sew the triangles together along the tops.

Note: For a no-sew variation, use a hot glue gun to glue the stained glass triangles along a ribbon.

MELTED-BEAD SUNCATCHERS

Melted-bead suncatchers are surprisingly easy to create yet very durable. Unlike the melted-crayon suncatchers, these suncatchers will withstand the elements for extended outdoor use.

MATERIALS

Translucent plastic pony beads
Old metal baking dishes such as muffin tins and cake pans
Grill or toaster oven
Power drill or metal grommets (see note below)
String

INSTRUCTIONS

1. Arrange the pony beads in a single layer in old metal baking dishes. You can also use old metal cookie cutters on a metal dish to create specific shapes.
2. Place the baking dishes on a hot grill for 5–15 minutes or until the beads are melted (start checking after 5 minutes). This is best done outdoors because of the plastic fumes; if you don't have a grill, consider using a toaster oven outside.
3. Let the melted beads cool completely, then pop the suncatchers out of the pans.
4. Drill a small hole in each suncatcher, tie some string through the hole, and use the loop to hang up your new suncatcher. You can create individual suncatchers or try connecting several together.

Note: If you don't have a power drill, include a metal grommet among the beads before melting them. The plastic beads will melt around the grommet, leaving the grommet hole open. (Thanks to one of my blog readers for the suggestion.)

MELTED-BEAD SUNCATCHER MOBILE

A mobile made out of colorful suncatchers is perfect for a child's room or a sunny window.

MATERIALS

Power drill or metal grommets (see note on page 128)
Small melted-bead suncatcher shapes made with muffin tins or cookie cutters (see page 128)
Large melted-bead suncatcher, made with a cake pan or similar (see page 128)
String

INSTRUCTIONS

1. Drill a hole near the top of each small melted-bead suncatcher shape. Drill four to six holes equidistant around the circumference of the large melted-bead suncatcher and one in its center.

2. To hang the suncatcher, loop and tie a length of string 1'–2' long through each of the holes along the edge of the large disk. Pull the strings together at the top and tie them into a knot. Hang the suncatcher up for the next step.

3. String two or three of the smaller shapes together and tie the end of the string to the large disk through the same hole as the hanging strips at the top and knot them, letting the shapes hang down. Repeat with the rest of the suncatcher shapes.

A SUNCATCHER GARLAND

String melted-bead suncatchers together to create a unique and lovely garland that works as well outside (it's waterproof) as in.

MATERIALS

Translucent pony beads (although any bead will do)
String, such as embroidery floss or kite string
Large needles, such as embroidery needles
Melted-bead suncatchers (page 128)

INSTRUCTIONS

1. Thread the needle with embroidery floss, then string pony beads on, tying a knot around the first to hold the rest on as you work.

2. Tie melted-bead suncatchers to the beaded string at regular intervals using embroidery floss. (For long garlands, you can make shorter sections and then tie several together, as we did.)

3. Hang the garland on a porch, in a window, or between poles in the garden. To enjoy the suncatchers at night, hang them alongside a string of white lights.

An indoor hopscotch can keep kids active on rainy days or when it's just too hot for outdoor play.

MATERIALS

Masking tape, rainbow colors optional (Test first to make sure the tape pulls up off your floor easily—it will in most cases.)
Melted-Crayon Rocks (see page 42) or other hopscotch marker

INSTRUCTIONS

1. Use masking tape to form hopscotch squares, numbering them with tape as you go. You can stick with the traditional 10, or you can go as high as you like. Ours reaches 27 and curves through three rooms.
2. Teach your kids how to play with a marker (see instructions below) or let them just jump along the course. Younger kids might not be quite ready for the official game, but the course itself is wonderful for balancing, coordination, and number recognition.

How to Play Hopscotch

1. Standing just in front of the hopscotch course, throw a hopscotch marker (melted-crayon rock, beanbag, or other small object) into the first square. If it lands on or outside the line, the player skips her turn.
2. If the marker lands inside the square, the player hops along the entire course, skipping the square with the stone. The player hops on one foot when there is a single square and hops onto both feet when there are two squares side by side, with one foot inside each square. If the player hops on the wrong square, touches the lines, or hops outside of a square, the player loses her turn and has to repeat that square on her next turn.

3. When the last square is reached, the player turns around and hops back through the course, pausing to pick up the marker on the way back.
4. Player hands the marker to the next player for his turn.

5. When it's the first player's turn again, she throws the marker to the second square and hops the course as before. The game continues until one player makes it through the entire course with the marker on each square.

GLUE BATIK FLAGS

Kids can make their own simple flags for Independence Day or pretend play.

MATERIALS

Scissors
White cotton fabric
Elmer's blue gel glue
Splat mat or wax paper
Paintbrushes
Acrylic paint
Scrub brush
Iron
Ironing board
Sewing machine (optional)
Wood dowel or bamboo pole
Stick-on Velcro tabs

INSTRUCTIONS

1. Cut the white fabric into the desired size and shape.
2. Squeeze the glue onto the fabric in the stars and stripes of the American flag (or any design). Let the glue dry.
3. Set your flag on a waterproof splat mat or a piece of wax paper. Paint with watered-down acrylic paints (about half and half works well). Let the paint dry.
4. Soak the flag in warm water for 30–60 minutes. Scrub the glue off with the brush. Let the flag dry, then iron it flat.
5. If desired, hem the edges or use a zigzag stitch around the edge to keep the flag from fraying.
6. Attach the flag to a dowel using sticky-back Velcro, and fly it. Have a backyard parade with your new flags or use them to decorate a sandbox, playhouse, or patio.

Summer Eating

In the summer we eat fruit like there's no tomorrow. We always try to eat seasonally for the most part (and the food tastes much better that way), so we take advantage of the fruit season to the hilt.

I have fond memories of picking blackberries as a child along our neighbor Wanda's long dirt driveway in the Oregon countryside. Many berries went straight into the mouth, but there were always enough for cobbler afterward. Now we take our own children berry picking at local farms, later enjoying the bounty in a variety of fresh and baked goods, and freezing the excess for the rest of the year.

OUR FAVORITE BOOKS ABOUT SUMMER FOOD

Blueberries for Sal by Robert McCloskey
Apple Pie 4th of July by Janet S. Wong

FRUIT GELATIN MOLD

This fruit gelatin is fresh, tasty, and perfectly refreshing as a dessert or snack on the hottest of summer days. This recipe is my attempt to re-create a favorite summer treat from my childhood.

INGREDIENTS

3-plus cups fresh fruit, such as grapes, peaches, kiwi, strawberries, blackberries (reserve some for garnish)
4 packets gelatin
6 cups cold cranberry juice
Mint (optional)

INSTRUCTIONS

1. Arrange the fresh fruit around the circumference of a Bundt pan. Set the pan aside.
2. Sprinkle the gelatin powder over 1 cup of the cold cranberry juice in a large bowl. Let it sit for 5 minutes.
3. Meanwhile, bring the remaining 5 cups of cranberry juice to a boil in a medium saucepan. Whisk the hot juice into the gelatin mixture. Let the gelatin cool to room temperature (I put the bowl in the fridge for 30–40 minutes), then pour the gelatin over the fruit in the Bundt pan. Cover the pan with plastic wrap and refrigerate overnight or until the gelatin is firm.
4. To release the mold from the pan, set the Bundt pan in a sink of warm water for 10–20 seconds or so. Then hold a large plate firmly over the top of the pan and invert them quickly.
5. Slice the gelatin and serve. Garnish it with fresh fruit and mint as desired.

BLUEBERRY HAND PIES

Blueberry pie goodness in a portable, little-person size.
Makes 14–16 hand pies

INGREDIENTS

1 batch Piecrust dough (see page 142)
1½ cups blueberries, fresh or frozen
¼ cup sugar, plus extra for sprinkling
2 tablespoons cornstarch
1 teaspoon lemon zest
1 tablespoon lemon juice
½ teaspoon vanilla
Pinch nutmeg
Egg wash (1 egg beaten with 1 tablespoon water)

INSTRUCTIONS

1. Preheat the oven to 375°F and line one or two cookie sheets with baking parchment. Bring the piecrust dough out of the fridge to soften slightly (about 15 minutes).

2. Mix together the blueberries, sugar, cornstarch, lemon zest, lemon juice, vanilla, and nutmeg.

3. Roll out half of the crust at a time on a floured surface. Use a 3" round biscuit or cookie cutter to cut rounds out of the dough. Transfer half of the dough rounds to the baking parchment–lined cookie sheets.

4. Add a spoonful of blueberry filling to the center of each round.

5. Cover each pie with a second round of dough. (You may want to roll out the top rounds a second time after you cut them out, to make them a bit bigger for better coverage.) Press the edges closed with fork tines.

6. Use a sharp knife to cut three or four little air vents in the top crusts. Brush each with egg wash, then sprinkle them with sugar.

7. Bake for 25 minutes or until the crust is golden brown at the edges. Eat warm or at room temperature.

PIECRUST

A good piecrust is key when making pies and hand pies.

INGREDIENTS

3 cups flour (I use half white whole wheat flour and half all-purpose flour.)
½ teaspoon salt
2 tablespoons sugar
1 cup (2 sticks) butter, sliced into tablespoons
12 tablespoons ice water

INSTRUCTIONS

1. Mix the dry ingredients in a food processor. Add half of the butter slices, pulse a couple times, then add the other half. Pulse several times. Alternatively, cut the butter into pea-size pieces with a pastry cutter or knife and fork.

2. Place the flour mixture in a large bowl. Add ice water 3 tablespoons at a time, using a sturdy rubber spatula to alternately mix and press down on the dough between water additions. Use the spatula or your hands to bring the dough into a loose ball.

3. Divide the dough in two and wrap each section in plastic wrap. Knead slightly through the wrap to create a more cohesive ball. Chill the dough in the fridge for at least 30 minutes. Follow individual recipes for uses and baking times.

FRUIT SPARKLERS

Make a summer snack sculpture inspired by fireworks and sparklers. Perfect for the Fourth of July or anytime.

INGREDIENTS

Banana
Fresh fruit, such as strawberries, grapes, blueberries, and blackberries
Wood skewers or toothpicks

INSTRUCTIONS

1. Place half of a peeled banana upright in a glass (to support the sparkler). Poke the end of a wood skewer or toothpick into the banana and then thread the skewer with a variety of berries and small fruits. Continue adding more skewers and fruit.
2. When the fruit sparkler is finished, admire it and then eat it.

HOMEMADE GRANOLA

Filled with delicious and healthy ingredients, this granola makes for a quick breakfast when you'd rather head outside than cook. I've adapted it from my friend Bobbi's recipe.

INGREDIENTS

4 cups old-fashioned rolled oats
1 cup unsweetened, shredded coconut
2–3 cups mixed, chopped nuts and seeds
1 teaspoon salt
1 teaspoon cinnamon
¾ teaspoon ground nutmeg
½ cup maple syrup
½ cup coconut oil
2 tablespoons honey
1 tablespoon vanilla
1–2 cups mixed dried berries and fruit
¼ cup ground flaxseed (optional)
Fresh fruit and yogurt or milk, for serving

INSTRUCTIONS

1. Preheat the oven to 325°F.
2. Mix the oats, dried coconut, nuts, salt, cinnamon, and nutmeg in a large bowl.
3. Whisk the syrup with the coconut oil (melt it first if it's solid). Stir in the honey and vanilla.
4. Pour the oil mixture into the oat mixture and stir until it's combined. Spread the mixture evenly in a large baking dish.
5. Bake the mixture, stirring it every 20 minutes or so, until it is toasted. It may take an hour or more, depending on how toasty you like it.
6. Let the granola cool, then stir in the dried fruit and the flaxseed, if desired. Store the granola covered in the fridge.
7. Serve the granola with fresh fruit and yogurt or milk.

FRESH-SQUEEZED LEMONADE

Nothing says summer quite as well as fresh-squeezed lemonade (and lemonade stands). Pairing sweet and sour, lemonade is refreshing on hot summer days. If you're feeling adventurous, you can even flavor it with the addition of fruits or herbs (our favorite variation is raspberry lemonade) or make frozen Popsicles with any extra.

INGREDIENTS

1 bag lemons
Simple syrup (see note below)
Ice cubes
Water

INSTRUCTIONS

1. Squeeze the lemons, straining out any seeds from the juice. Measure the lemon juice and pour it into a pitcher.

2. Add an equal amount of simple syrup to the lemon juice.

3. Fill the rest of the pitcher with ice and water. Stir and serve.

Note: To make simple syrup, mix 1 cup sugar with 1 cup water in a small saucepan and bring it to a boil. Stir the mixture until the sugar dissolves completely. Let the syrup cool, then store it covered in the fridge.

VARIATION

To add a fruity kick and color (such as for raspberry lemonade), puree fresh or frozen fruit in a blender, strain it through a fine sieve, then stir the fruit puree into the lemonade.

FRUIT NECKLACES

String fruit into an edible (and healthy) necklace for a fun activity and snack.

INGREDIENTS

Elastic thread or string
Yarn needle
Fruit, such as strawberries, blueberries, and grapes

INSTRUCTIONS

1. Thread elastic thread or regular string through an embroidery or yarn needle. Tie a knot near the other end to hold all the fruit beads on the necklace.

2. Poke the needle through a grape (or other piece of fruit) and push it to the knotted end.

3. Continue stringing the fruit beads onto the necklace in patterns or as desired. Tie the two ends of the elastic thread together when the necklace is complete.

4. Wear, admire, and snack on your edible jewelry.

FRUIT POPSICLES

Puree fruit and juice in a variety of tasty combinations for healthy, DIY frozen treats that kids love. Try these flavor combinations or make up your own: strawberries with orange juice and a spoonful of honey, blueberries with coconut milk, mango with yogurt, pineapple and banana with coconut milk.

INGREDIENTS

2 cups fresh or frozen fruit
1 cup juice, yogurt, or coconut milk
Popsicle molds

INSTRUCTIONS

1. Place the fruit and juice in a blender. Blend until smooth.
2. Pour the mixture into Popsicle molds.
3. Freeze the Popsicles until they're frozen solid.
4. To remove the Popsicles, run the mold under warm water briefly, then pull each Popsicle out.
5. Enjoy these refreshing Popsicles on a hot day.

MIXED-BERRY SCONES WITH LEMON ICING

Bursting with flavor from the berries and lemon, these scones are a tasty weekend treat.

For the Scones

1 cup white whole wheat flour
1 cup all-purpose flour
¼ cup sugar
1 tablespoon baking powder
½ teaspoon salt
Zest from 1 lemon
6 tablespoons butter, sliced
1 egg
½ cup plain or vanilla yogurt (I use whole-milk yogurt)
1–2 cups fresh or frozen berries, such as blackberries, raspberries, strawberries, and blueberries

For the Lemon Icing

1 tablespoon lemon juice
1 cup powdered sugar

INSTRUCTIONS

1. Preheat the oven to 425°F. Line a cookie sheet with baking parchment.
2. Measure all the dry ingredients, including the lemon zest, into a food processor. Run for a minute to mix.
3. Add the butter pieces to the flour mixture. Pulse several times until the butter is pea size or smaller. (Or you can just mix the dry ingredients and then cut the butter into them using a pastry blender or knife and fork.) Transfer the mixture to a large bowl.

4. Whisk together the egg and yogurt. Make a well in the center of the flour and pour in the egg mixture. Stir the batter until it's combined and the dough starts to come together.
5. Fold in the berries.
6. Turn the dough out onto the counter and shape it into a disk about 1" thick. Cut it, like a pie, into eight wedges.
7. Bake the scones for 20 minutes or until they're cooked through and toasty brown on the edges. Let them cool slightly.
8. Make the lemon icing by whisking the ingredients together. Drizzle the icing over the scones. Serve warm or at room temperature.

COCONUT CHICKEN SATAY WITH MANGO SAUCE

This is a tasty summer staple that can be cooked on the grill, over an open fire, or in the oven. A side of steamed rice is a nice accompaniment. *Note:* The chicken will need to marinate for 2–3 hours before grilling.

Serves 6–8

INGREDIENTS

1 can coconut milk (about 14 oz.)
Zest and juice from two limes
¼ cup light brown sugar
1 tablespoon sea salt
2 garlic cloves, minced
2 teaspoons fresh ginger, grated
1½ pounds boneless, skinless chicken breasts, cut into strips
½ teaspoon turmeric
1 mango

To Serve

1 head lettuce with large leaves (butter lettuce works well)
Mango coconut sauce
½ cup cilantro, chopped
½ cup roasted and salted peanuts, chopped
½ cup chopped scallions (optional)

INSTRUCTIONS

1. Whisk together the coconut milk, lime zest and juice, brown sugar, sea salt, garlic, and ginger in a medium bowl. Remove ½ cup of the coconut mixture and set it aside. Add the chicken strips and turmeric to the remaining coconut mixture in the bowl and toss until the chicken is fully coated in the marinade. Cover and refrigerate for 2–3 hours.

2. Score the outside of the mango with a knife, then bend the skin back so the cubed flesh sticks up. Slice off the skin from the cubes.

3. Puree the mango cubes with the ½ cup reserved coconut mixture in a blender or food processor. Cover the mango coconut sauce and refrigerate it until ready to serve.

4. When the chicken has finished marinating, thread it onto wood skewers that have been soaked in water for half an hour, or use metal skewers.

5. Grill the chicken over medium-high heat, about 4–5 minutes on each side, until the chicken is cooked through. If you're using an oven, broil the chicken for 4–5 minutes on each side. Check for doneness by piercing the thickest piece of chicken. It should be opaque in the center.

6. To serve, place a large lettuce leaf on each plate. Slide some chicken off a skewer and onto the lettuce. Top the chicken with a spoonful or two of mango coconut sauce, cilantro, and a sprinkle of roasted peanuts. Add scallions if desired. Fold the lettuce over the fillings, like a burrito, and enjoy.

QUINOA TABBOULEH WITH ADDITIONAL MIX-INS

This summer favorite combines the refreshing flavors of traditional tabbouleh, replacing the bulgur wheat with protein-rich quinoa. We like to make a large batch and keep it in the fridge as an easy, chilled snack or meal for when it's just too hot to cook. While tabbouleh is great as it is, we often add extras or make substitutions as our garden, fridge, and whims decree.

Serves 8–10

BASIC INGREDIENTS

1 cup quinoa
1½ cups water
1 tablespoon sea salt
¼ cup olive oil
Juice from 2 lemons
Freshly ground black pepper, to taste
1 large cucumber, peeled and chopped
2 cups cherry tomatoes, halved
1 bunch scallions, sliced
1 cup fresh mint, chopped
1 cup fresh flat-leaf parsley, chopped

Ideas for Additional Mix-Ins

1–2 cups cubed, grilled chicken
1 cup cubed or crumbled feta cheese
1–2 cups canned chickpeas
1–2 cups grapes, halved
1–2 cups slivered almonds
1 cup roasted beets, cubed
1 cup boiled or roasted potatoes, cubed

1. Place the quinoa in a medium pot with a lid. Cover the quinoa with water and soak it for half an hour. Carefully pour off the soaking water and rinse the quinoa two or three times or until the water is relatively clear. Drain well and return the quinoa to the pot.

2. Add the water and ½ teaspoon of the salt. Bring the water to a boil. Turn the heat down to low. Simmer, covered, for 20 minutes.

3. Place the cooked quinoa in a large bowl and toss it with the olive oil, lemon juice, the remaining salt, and pepper. Set the quinoa aside while you chop the vegetables and herbs.

4. Add the vegetables, herbs, and any extra mix-ins and toss them to combine. Cover the tabbouleh and refrigerate it for a few hours or overnight to let the flavors combine. Serve the tabbouleh at room temperature or chilled.

CRANBERRY GRANOLA BARS

These granola bars are healthy, yummy, and great for breakfast on the go or a quick snack. My children love them in their school lunches, too.

Makes about 30 bars

INGREDIENTS

2 cups old-fashioned rolled oats
1 cup almond meal
½ cup whole wheat flour
1 teaspoon cinnamon
1 teaspoon salt
1 cup dried cranberries
⅓ cup mini chocolate chips
½ cup (1 stick) butter
½ cup honey
1 egg
2 teaspoons vanilla

INSTRUCTIONS

1. Preheat the oven to 350°F. Line a 9" x 13" baking pan with baking parchment.
2. Mix the oats, almond meal, flour, cinnamon, salt, cranberries, and chocolate chips in a large bowl.
3. Melt the butter in a small saucepan. Whisk in the honey, then the egg and vanilla. Pour the butter mixture into the oat mixture and combine thoroughly.
4. Press the dough into the pan and bake for 20–25 minutes.
5. Cool the baked dough partially, then cut it into bars. Store the bars, wrapped, in the fridge or freezer.

Backyard Creativity

Longer summer days and inviting warm weather create an emphasis on outdoor living and connecting with nature. At my house, we go outside to play, garden, dine, and entertain. We cook our dinners on the grill or over the fire pit, eat on the patio, hike through the woods, have picnics (everywhere), splash in the pool, and run through the sprinkler. Our children practice cartwheels and handstands by the dozen, spend hours on the swing, decorate our walkways and stones with chalk, and create miniature worlds in the sandbox.

OUR FAVORITE BOOKS ABOUT SUMMER ADVENTURES

Weslandia by Paul Fleischman
Grandma Summer by Harley Jessup
Roxaboxen by Alice McLerran
How I Spent My Summer Vacation by Mark Teague
A Camping Spree with Mr. Magee by Chris Van Dusen
You Can't Take a Balloon into the Metropolitan Museum by Jacqueline Preiss Weitzman

FLOWER NECKLACES

Children love to string their own flower necklaces, bracelets, and crowns out of marigolds and other flowers.

MATERIALS

Flowers such as marigolds or zinnias
Embroidery needle
Embroidery floss

1. Pick flower heads, such as marigolds or zinnias.
2. Thread a large embroidery needle with embroidery floss and tie a knot at the end.
3. String the flowers by poking the needle through the fleshy flower base (on marigolds) or through the center of the flower (on zinnias). Continue until the flower necklace is the desired length, then tie the ends together. Wear and show off your flower necklace.

SANDBOX CAKES

A bit cleaner than mud pies, sandbox cakes are just as popular with kids and are readily decorated with items found around the garden.

MATERIALS

Small shovel or large spoon
Old cake pans, muffin tins, and jelly molds
Sandbox
Nature items, such as flowers, pebbles, twigs, and pinecones
Melted-crayon rocks (see page 42, optional)

INSTRUCTIONS

1. Use the shovel or spoon to fill the cake pans and other molds with sand from the sandbox. Decorate the sand cakes with nature items and melted-crayon rocks, if desired.

2. Have a sand-cake tea party.

This is a fun and simple art project for the beach or sandbox.

MATERIALS

Bottle of glue
Card stock or heavy paper, white or colored
Sand (from sandbox or beach)
Paint (tempera, watercolor, BioColor, or acrylic) and paintbrush (optional)

INSTRUCTIONS

1. Squeeze some glue onto the card stock to create pictures or designs.
2. Sprinkle a light layer of sand over the glue picture, then shake off the excess. Repeat if necessary until you've coated the glue completely with sand. Let the glue dry.
3. If desired, paint over the dried sand picture. You can also paint just on the paper or just on the sand lines.

SAND-CASTING

Sand-casting is a fun activity for the beach or the sandbox and creates a special memento filled with treasures.

MATERIALS

Shovel
Sand (beach or sandbox)
Small nature items, such as shells, pebbles, flowers, sticks
Small treasures, such as glass beads, marbles, little figurines (optional)
Melted-crayon rocks, optional (see page 42)
Plaster of Paris
Old bucket and spoon for mixing the plaster
Water

INSTRUCTIONS

1. Dig a hole in the sand.
2. Line the hole with your treasures (shells, rocks, glass beads, marbles, melted crayon rocks, and so on).
3. Mix the plaster of Paris in the old bucket, using 2 parts plaster to 1 part water.
4. Pour the wet plaster into the holes, covering the treasures and filling the holes.
5. Optional step: decorate the tops by poking in more treasures.
6. Let the plaster sit for 30 minutes or so, to set it.
7. Lift the sand cast out of the sand, turn it over, and carefully dust off the extra sand. Place it in a protected place overnight to continue the drying process.
8. Display your sand-casted plaster on the summer nature table or mantel.

SAND-CAST CANDLEHOLDERS

Bring beach magic to everyday life with sand-casted candleholders.

MATERIALS

Shovel
Sand (beach or sandbox)
Glass votive holders
Shells, pebbles, glass beads, and other treasures
Plaster of Paris
Water
Old bucket and spoon for mixing the plaster
Votive candles or tealights

INSTRUCTIONS

1. Dig a hole in the sand at least as deep as your votive holder.
2. Set the glass votive holder upside down at the bottom of the hole.
3. Arrange shells, pebbles, glass beads, and other treasures around the rim of the votive holder and around the edge of the hole.
4. Mix and pour the plaster of Paris, following steps 3–7 for sand-casting (see page 163).
5. Add a votive candle or tealight and enjoy the candlelight and treasurescape together.

SAND TATTOOS

These temporary tattoos are unique and a fun DIY project for summer.

MATERIALS

Bottle of glue
Sand

INSTRUCTIONS

Squeeze glue into a picture or design on your skin. Sprinkle sand over the glue and shake off the excess. The tattoo washes off with soap and water.

CHALK PAINT

Mix up a quick batch of chalk paint and let the kids paint rocks, the patio, and the sidewalk.

MATERIALS

Large spoon
Cornstarch
Water
Medium bowl
Cups
Tempera paint or food coloring
Paintbrush

INSTRUCTIONS

1. Mix equal parts of cornstarch and water in the bowl. (It will be hard to stir. Just do your best.)

2. Divide the cornstarch mixture between individual cups, then stir in enough tempera paint or food coloring to reach the color intensity desired.

3. Paint the world! The chalk paint washes away with rain or the spray of a hose.

BEADED BUBBLE WANDS

Kids will love making their own (beautiful) beaded bubble wands. This makes a great party or play-date activity.

MATERIALS

Pipe cleaners
Small wooden dowels (or cut a long one into sections)
Assorted beads
Hot glue gun
Bubble solution (see page 169)

INSTRUCTIONS

1. Twist one end of a pipe cleaner around the tip of a dowel.
2. Thread beads along the pipe cleaner, leaving an inch or so clear.
3. Bend the beaded pipe cleaner into a loop and twist the end around the dowel. Add a dab of glue from the hot glue gun to help hold the pipe cleaner in place.
4. Dip the beaded bubble wand in the bubble solution and blow through it or wave it through the air to make magical bubbles.

HOMEMADE BUBBLES

No need to fear running out of bubbles when you can make your own so easily.

MATERIALS

½ cup sugar
4 cups warm water
½ cup dish soap (Dawn original dish soap works best.)

INSTRUCTIONS

Whisk the sugar in the warm water until it's dissolved. Stir in the dish soap. Blow bubbles!

QUICK BACKYARD TEEPEE

Quick to put up, this teepee becomes a shady backyard spot for playing, reading, and eating.

MATERIALS

2" x 2" wood poles or boards, 8'–10' long
Large tree (optional)
Rope
Old sheets or tablecloths
Large safety pins
Rugs or blankets (optional)

INSTRUCTIONS

1. Prop poles against and around the tree trunk at a 45-degree angle, creating a teepee shape. Lash the poles to the tree with rope. (Alternatively, create a freestanding teepee by tying the tops of the poles together.)

2. Drape tablecloths or sheets over the teepee structure, holding the fabric in place by wrapping it around the poles and fastening it with safety pins.

3. Cover the floor of the teepee with old rugs or blankets if desired.

AUTUMN

I'm so glad I live in a world where
there are Octobers.

—*ANNE OF GREEN GABLES*

AUTUMN PROJECTS

CELEBRATING AUTUMN

YOU KNOW HOW YOU CAN just feel the fall coming, by the hints in the air, as before a storm? I revel in the cooling-down sights and smells of autumn and the feeling of getting ready to nestle inside where it's warm and cozy.

The breathtaking fall foliage, apple picking (and apple cider doughnuts), acorn collecting, pumpkins everywhere, crisp air, harvest foods, and Halloween excitement all get me in the mood to craft, celebrate, decorate, and bake.

As with each season, my family and I celebrate by spending time together, taking nature walks to observe the changes outdoors, making holiday crafts and decorations, and cooking up seasonal foods in the kitchen.

Autumn-Leaf Crafts

Autumn carries more gold in its pocket than all the other seasons.

—JIM BISHOP

Spectacular autumn leaves make the flowers we loved so much earlier in the year pale by comparison. Their stately beauty pushes everything else aside, taking the forefront during their brief season of splendor. It's as though the trees had waited all year for their turn onstage. The early spring daffodils are distant memories and the billowy hibiscus forgotten.

We take foliage drives through the countryside. We gather and press red, yellow, and orange leaves to use in our crafts and decorations, including nature suncatchers and doodle leaf art, and in family games.

PRESSING AUTUMN LEAVES

There are many, many crafts using the colorful leaves of autumn. Most work better with leaves that are first pressed and dried so that they are flat and the color and shape are better preserved. Here are two methods, one that takes 1–2 weeks and one that takes a few minutes.

FOR THE TRADITIONALIST

I press and dry my leaves the traditional way—between the pages of a phone book. That's what it's for, right? If I didn't think ahead and I've already recycled our phone book, I use any book. Put the leaves between cheap copy paper or paper from the recycle bin in order to protect the pages of the book and place the leaves inside. Of course you can use a flower press if you have one (we do, and yet I still use the phone book).

Set the phone book under a few heavy books and forget about the leaves for 1 or, ideally, 2 weeks. When you take them out, they should be flat and dry. You're ready to get crafting.

THE MICROWAVE METHOD

Alternatively, you can use the microwave to press and dry your autumn leaves in minutes instead of days or weeks. Here's how.

On your microwave turntable, layer 3 paper towels, the leaves you want to dry (spread out so they don't touch), 3 more paper towels, and a plate to hold it all in place. Microwave on medium for 30 seconds. Check for dryness. If the leaves need more time, microwave them for another 30 seconds, and then possibly another. Watch carefully and don't let them get overdry (there is potential for fire if you let them dry too much).

LEAF DOODLES

Leaves prove to be a lovely seasonal canvas for small drawings and doodles.

MATERIALS

Autumn leaves, pressed and dried (see page 176)
Metallic Sharpie markers
Wax paper
Foam brush (a regular paintbrush will work okay too)
Mod Podge

INSTRUCTIONS

1. Doodle and draw on your leaves with the metallic Sharpies. Try tracing the veins, drawing pictures, writing words, or making mandalas.
2. Spread your leaves out on a sheet of wax paper.
3. Brush a layer of Mod Podge over the tops of the leaves. Let them dry. Turn the leaves over and brush a layer of Mod Podge across the bottom of the leaves.
4. Let the leaves dry completely, then use them for autumn decorations or gifts (see the Autumn Leaf Mandala on page 180 or the Thanksgiving Leaf Banner on page 234).

AUTUMN LEAF MANDALAS

Create nature art on your walls with colorful autumn leaves.

MATERIALS

Wall putty or a glue stick

Doodled leaves from the previous activity or plain pressed and dried autumn leaves (see page 176)

INSTRUCTIONS

1. Use little pieces of the wall putty to stick doodled leaves on the wall—or dabs from a glue stick to adhere leaves to a window—in a radiating mandala design. (Wall putty can be easily removed and it leaves no stain; glue washes off windows easily.)

2. Reposition the leaves as desired over time to create new mandalas and other designs.

PAINTED PAPER LEAVES

Besides creating arts and crafts with real leaves, we can take inspiration from nature and paint our own autumn leaves.

MATERIALS

Waterproof tablecloth, place mat, or newspaper
Droppers or paintbrushes
Paper leaves (see note below)
Liquid watercolors in fall colors

INSTRUCTIONS

1. Protect your work surface with a waterproof tablecloth, place mat, or newspaper (the paint soaks through the paper leaves and is not completely washable).
2. Use droppers or brushes to transfer the watercolor paint to the paper leaves. Try more than one color per leaf and watch as the paint colors spread and merge.
3. Let the leaves dry. Hang them on a paper tree (see page 182) in a window or create a garland with them.

Note: Precut leaves can be purchased (see the resources section), or cut your own from coffee filters or paper using the leaf templates on page 329.

VARIATIONS

- Draw veins (or any pictures, designs, and so on) on the paper leaves first with crayons or oil pastels, then paint over the picture for a watercolor-resist effect. (The wax and oil of crayons and oil pastels prevent the water-based paint from adhering. This technique is especially effective with a white or light-colored crayon and a darker paint.)
- Do a leaf rubbing on the paper leaf first with the side of a crayon (place a real leaf under the paper leaf), then paint.
- Use a dropper to paint a leaf with a generous amount of watercolor paint, then sprinkle it with salt. Leave the salt on until the leaf is dry, then rub it off.

A BROWN-PAPER TREE

Bring autumn inside (and provide a display for all of your leaf art) with a tree made of paper.

MATERIALS

Scissors
Contractor's paper (see resources section) or brown craft paper
Black masking tape (make sure it's easily removable; don't use electrical tape)
Paper leaves or doodled leaves (see pages 181 and 178)

INSTRUCTIONS

1. Cut a tree trunk from the brown contractor's paper (draw it first if you like, or just wing it).

2. Tape the tree trunk on your wall with the black masking tape. This not only attaches it to the wall but also gives it a nice crisp outline.

3. Cut branches from the paper and tape them up as well. Continue to cut and tape until you are happy with how your tree looks.

4. Add fall foliage to your tree with paper leaves, doodled leaves, or a combination of the two.

LEAF-RUBBINGS STAINED GLASS

Leaf rubbings are a classic childhood art activity that reveal the intricate vein designs of a variety of leaves. This stained glass project takes the idea to another level, creating beautiful art best displayed with light shining through it.

MATERIALS

Assortment of leaves (the fresher and less dry, the better)

Easel paper

Tape

Crayons with the paper removed (we use chunky crayons, but any size works fine)

Paintbrush

Watercolors (liquid watercolors work great)

Scissors

Vegetable oil

INSTRUCTIONS

1. Spread the leaves out on a table, vein side up.
2. Place a sheet of the easel paper over the leaves and tape it down.
3. Rub across the paper, gently but firmly, with the side of a crayon. Repeat with other colors as desired.
4. Paint over the crayon rubbings with watercolors. Let the paint dry.
5. Cut the paper into pieces to fit your windowpanes.
6. Paint the uncolored side of the leaf rubbings with a light coating of vegetable oil.
7. Press the stained glass panels to your window. The oil will make them stick by themselves.

PLASTER LEAF CASTS

These leaf casts are fairly delicate, and some of the thinner ones may crack if not handled with care. They look amazing, though, and are worth making anyway. I would suggest putting them where you can enjoy looking at them but where they won't be handled regularly.

MATERIALS

Large leaves (fresh and flexible rather than dry and brittle)
Wax paper
Oil spray (used for cooking), such as Pam
2 cups water
½ cup white school glue
5 cups plaster of Paris
Resealable gallon-size plastic bags
Scissors
BioColor paint or metallic liquid watercolors (optional)

INSTRUCTIONS

1. Lay your leaves down, vein side up, on a sheet of wax paper on the grass outside (for a more rounded cast) or on a table inside (for a flatter cast). Spray the leaves with a light coating of oil.

2. Whisk together the water and glue in a bowl.

3. Measure the plaster of Paris into the resealable plastic bag. Pour in the water-glue mixture. Close the bag securely and squeeze it and squish it until the plaster is well mixed.

4. Use scissors to remove one corner of the bag. You'll squeeze the plaster out of that opening (as with a pastry bag).

5. Working fairly quickly (before the plaster hardens), squeeze the plaster out onto a leaf and spread it to the edges of the leaf with the back of a spoon.

6. Repeat with more leaves as desired.

If you need to mix up more plaster of Paris (use a fresh bag), the ratio is 2 parts plaster to 1 part water-glue mixture.

7. Let the plaster harden for 1–2 hours before moving your leaves to a place to cure for 1–2 days.

8. Turn each cast over and remove the leaf. Some leaves pull off easily and quickly and some come off in pieces. Use a nail brush (gently), a toothpick, or tweezers for any difficult-to-remove parts.

9. Paint the leaves with BioColor paint in fall colors if desired. Let the paint dry.

10. Use the leaves as part of a fall nature table, mantelpiece decoration, or table centerpiece.

MIXED-MEDIA AUTUMN TREES

Children enjoy combining multiple art techniques and materials in this fall leaf project.

MATERIALS

Paper
Colored masking tape
Scissors
Ink pad(s) (we used red, gold, and black)
Small fresh leaves (we used fresh sage leaves)
Glue
Small leaves pressed and dried (see page 176)

INSTRUCTIONS

1. Cut pieces of colored masking tape and press them onto the paper to create a bare tree.
2. Press the fresh leaves on the ink pad, then onto the paper to create leaf prints. Thumb- and fingerprints work pretty well, too.
3. Glue the dried leaves directly onto the tree, for a combination of leaves and leaf prints.

MELTED-CRAYON LEAVES

Decorate your window with colorful autumn leaves—made with crayon shavings and wax paper.

MATERIALS

Cheese grater
Crayons in red, yellow, orange, brown
Bowls or muffin tin
Iron
Wax paper
Ironing board
Newsprint or cheap copy paper
Scissors
Hole punch
Yarn or string (or glue stick)

INSTRUCTIONS

1. Follow steps 1–6 for the Melted-Crayon Suncatchers on page 23.
2. Cut leaf shapes out of the melted-crayon stained glass sheets. You can cut freehand or use the templates on page 329.
3. Punch a hole through the top of each leaf. String yarn through the hole and tie the ends together to create a loop to use for hanging the leaf in a sunny window. Or use a dab from a glue stick.

PAINTING ACORNS AND PINECONES

While acorns and pinecones are perfectly lovely in their natural state, they serve as unique canvases for paint and glitter.

MATERIALS

Tray or splat mat
Paintbrush
Paint (tempera, BioColor, or acrylic) in autumn colors
Pinecones
Acorns, baked first (see note below)
Glitter (optional)
Hot glue gun

INSTRUCTIONS

1. Protect your work surface with a tray or splat mat.
2. Paint the pinecones and acorns. Sprinkle the wet paint with glitter if desired.
3. If any acorn tops have become separated from the nuts, glue them back on.
4. Display the acorns and pinecones in a bowl or basket. Keep them accessible—kids love to handle them.

Note: Baking the acorns before using them for art or home decor prevents little maggots from burrowing out of them in a week or two. Gross, huh? I debated telling you this but thought you might skip this step if you didn't know the reason behind it. Learn from my mistake. To bake the acorns, spread them out in a single layer on a cookie sheet. Bake at 350°F for 15 minutes. Let them cool.

FELT-LEAF GARLAND

Upcycle old wool sweaters into an autumn-leaf garland that can be brought out to decorate the house year after year.

MATERIALS

One or more old wool sweaters in autumnal colors
Scissors
Sewing machine (optional)
Embroidery needle
Embroidery floss
Ribbon, ¼" wide, in length of desired garland

INSTRUCTIONS

1. First, felt the wool sweaters by washing them in a long hot-water cycle in the washing machine with soap and then drying them in the dryer.

2. Use the scissors to cut leaf shapes out of the felted wool. You can do this either freehand or by using the leaf templates on page 329.

3. Optional step: cut thin strips of contrasting felted wool and sew them down the center of each leaf with a sewing machine.

4. Thread the embroidery needle with embroidery floss and embroider basic veins on the felt leaves (see basic embroidery instructions on page 25).

5. Sew the leaves along the ribbon with an X stitch connecting the stem of each leaf to the ribbon at even intervals.

6. Hang the garland over a mantel, across a window, or anywhere you could use a little extra seasonal decoration.

Halloween

There is an air of excitement around Halloween, the holiday that allows us to try on different roles for a night (or if you're like my kids, for the weeks before and after). Personally, I can pass on the scarier sides of Halloween, but who doesn't have a little fun with bats, spiderwebs, ghosts, and witches?

We like the family-friendly versions of Halloween decor and festivities immensely, including, of course, the wonderful jack-o'-lanterns to carve and decorate. We visit the pick-your-own pumpkin patch and choose the just-right pumpkins that will grace our front porch.

Our dress-up box is in use year-round, but it gets extraspecial attention in the month or so preceding Halloween, when everyone asks my daughters, "What will you be?" All sorts of combinations and ideas are tried on. They take Halloween costumes as seriously as college grads considering career selection.

PAINTING PUMPKINS

A fun and festive way to decorate pumpkins that even the youngest kid can do.

MATERIALS

Paint (see note below)
Paintbrushes
Pumpkins

INSTRUCTIONS

1. Let kids paint their pumpkins as desired. Some may choose to paint the entire pumpkin, some may just add a few dabs. Some may use a brush; others, just their hands.
2. Let the pumpkins dry completely.
3. Display the painted pumpkins with pride.

Note: Activity paint and BioColor paint work great for this activity and adhere well to the pumpkins. Acrylics work well, too, but they are permanent on clothes, dry very quickly, and are not as kid-friendly. You can use tempera paint, but mix in a bit of dish soap first to make it stick. Black and white are especially effective Halloween colors.

JACK-O'-LANTERN CARVING FOR KIDS

Kids can carve pumpkins themselves with the right tools. Younger children, especially, may also enjoy using pushpins, nails, and other items to decorate the pumpkins.

MATERIALS

Paper
Marker or pencil
Pumpkin
Pumpkin carving kit (the cheap kind found everywhere, with the pulp scraper and little saws)
Candle

INSTRUCTIONS

1. Kids can practice their jack-o'-lantern faces on paper first to decide what kind of face they'd like on their pumpkin (the Fill in the Jack-o'-Lantern Faces activity on page 199 is good for this too).

2. Once they have decided on a face, they can draw the face directly on the pumpkin with a marker.

3. You can then cut off the top of the pumpkin, making sure to cut at an angle so that the top can rest in place securely.

4. Let your kids scoop out the pulp and pumpkin seeds (save the seeds if you like to roast them) from inside the pumpkin, using the pulp scraper if your kit includes one (it's very effective).

5. Using the small saw in the carving kit, carve out the jack-o'-lantern features. Depending on the age of the child, he may be able to do this without help or he may need some assistance.

6. Set a candle inside, light it, and enjoy the spooky (or friendly) glow of your jack-o'-lantern.

JACK-O'-LANTERN PLAYDOUGH

Kids love to poke black beans into playdough to form jack-o'-lantern faces.

MATERIALS

Pumpkin pie playdough recipe (see page 18) or other playdough
Dried black beans

INSTRUCTIONS

1. Form your playdough into pumpkin shapes.
2. Arrange and poke the dried black beans on the surface of the playdough pumpkin to form the jack-o'-lantern face. Toddlers love poking things into playdough and will likely poke the beans in randomly—that's okay, too.
3. Display the pumpkins, or remove the beans and store the playdough for another day.

FILL IN THE JACK-O'-LANTERN FACES

Invite kids to draw a variety of jack-o'-lantern faces by drawing simple pumpkin outlines for them. This is a great way to practice before carving a real pumpkin and can also be a fun Halloween party activity.

MATERIALS

Chalk or markers
Chalkboard or paper

INSTRUCTIONS

1. Draw several pumpkin outlines of varying shapes and sizes on the chalkboard or paper.

2. Invite your children to complete the jack-o'-lanterns by drawing the faces.

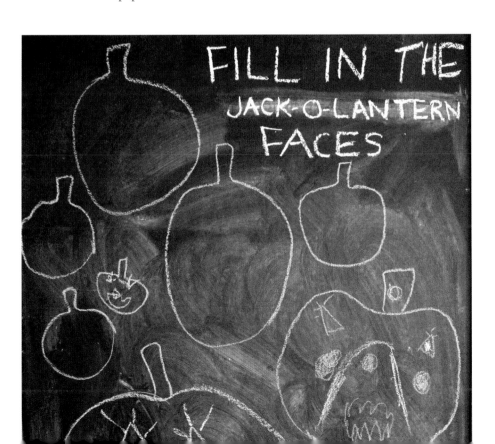

JACK-O'-LANTERN POINTILLISM

Try a simple pointillism technique to create jack-o'-lantern faces.

MATERIALS

Marker or crayon
Orange construction paper
Scissors
Q-tips
Black tempera paint (shallow puddle on a plate or in a small bowl)

INSTRUCTIONS

1. Draw a pumpkin shape on the construction paper and cut it out.
2. Dip a Q-tip into the black paint and paint multiple dots for the jack-o'-lantern facial features. Younger kids, especially, are likely to paint with the Q-tip instead. That's okay, too.

JACK-O'-LANTERN BLOTTO FACES

Learn about symmetry as you paint half a face and print the second half from the first.

MATERIALS

Drawing tool, such as a marker or crayon
Orange construction paper
Scissors
Paintbrush
Black paint

INSTRUCTIONS

1. Draw a large pumpkin on the orange paper. Cut it out.
2. Fold the pumpkin in half, with the crease going down the center of the stem. Open the pumpkin back up.
3. Paint half of a jack-o'-lantern face on one side of the pumpkin (one eye, half a nose, half a mouth).
4. Fold the pumpkin closed over the paint and press with your hands.
5. Open the paper to reveal your complete jack-o'-lantern face.

 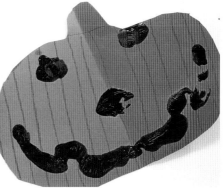

SPOOKY FUN FELT GARLANDS

Cut bats or jack-o'-lanterns out of felt and sew them together to form a garland. Hang your garland indoors or out (we especially like ours on the porch) to spookify your Halloween decor.

MATERIALS

For the Felt Jack-o'-Lantern Garland

Jack-o'-lantern template (see page 330 or draw your own)
Orange felt (by the yard is best)
Sharp scissors
Orange thread
Sewing machine or glue or stapler
Ribbon (optional)

For the Felt Bat Garland

Bat template (see page 330 or draw your own)
Sharp scissors
Black felt (by the yard is best for this project)
Black thread
Sewing machine

INSTRUCTIONS

1. To make the jack-o'-lantern garland, fold the template in half.
2. Fold the orange felt in half and line up the folded edge of the paper template with the folded edge of the felt. Use the template as a guide to cut out your felt jack-o'-lanterns. Do the same for each eye, or just cut the eyes without a template.
3. Using the orange thread, sew the felt jack-o'-lanterns together with a long running stitch on the sewing machine, leaving an inch or so between each pumpkin. Nonsewers can opt to glue or staple the pumpkin stems to a ribbon for their garland.

4. To make the bat garland, use your template to cut out as many bats from your black felt as you like.

5. Using the black thread, sew your bats together, wingtip to wingtip, with a continuous long stitch (I used a basting stitch) on the sewing machine. Leave extra thread at each end for hanging the garland.

YARN SPIDERWEBS

Fashion spiderwebs that will hold their shape out of yarn dipped in glue.

MATERIALS

Scissors
White yarn
White school glue, such as Elmer's
Medium bowl
Water
Wax paper

INSTRUCTIONS

1. Cut white yarn into lengths of 1'–2', depending on the desired diameter of the finished spiderweb.
2. Pour the glue into a medium bowl. Thin it with water (about 3 parts glue to 1 part water).
4. Cover your work surface with wax paper. To create the base of the spiderweb, dip a piece of yarn in the glue and then spread it out on the wax paper. Continue with several more lengths of yarn, crossing them over the first at the center like spokes in a wheel.
5. Once the base is complete, connect the radiating yarn pieces with additional lengths of glue-soaked yarn, spiraling around and around to create a spiderweb design. You can also curve the yarn between each spoke.
6. Let the yarn dry (this may take a couple of days), then turn the spiderweb over and pull off the wax paper. You'll have a yarn spiderweb that holds its shape.
7. Hang the spiderweb in a doorway, in a window, or on the wall. Alternatively, you can use it as the base of a table centerpiece.

POM-POM SPIDERS

Spiders for your yarn webs are easily created from pom-poms and pipe cleaners.

MATERIALS

Scissors
Black pipe cleaners
Hot glue gun
Black pom-poms in two sizes
Googly eyes (optional)

INSTRUCTIONS

1. Cut four pipe cleaners in half. Hold them together and use a small pipe cleaner piece to twist around the others at the center.
2. Bend each leg down at the middle, then up for the feet.
3. Use a hot glue gun to attach the pom-pom body and head to the center of the pipe cleaner leg assembly.
4. Use the spiders to decorate your home for Halloween. Add some to the yarn spiderwebs (see page 204) or create a line of spiders along your wall (try double-stick tape).

COFFEE FILTER SPIDERWEBS

These simple spiderwebs are created much the same way as paper snowflakes. Attach them to a window with a few dabs from a glue stick (it washes off easily when you're ready to remove them). You can even create small spiders for your webs out of black felt or black construction paper, gluing them to the coffee filter spiderwebs.

MATERIALS

White coffee filters (the basket filters rather than the cone kind)
Scissors

INSTRUCTIONS

1. Fold the coffee filter in half, then in half again (and again, too, if you'd like) into a triangle as when making a paper snowflake.
2. Use your scissors to cut horizontal lines across the folds of the coffee filter triangle, cutting out narrow triangles or rectangles.
3. Repeat with more coffee filters, trying a few different variations as desired.

MARBLE-ROLLING SPIDERWEBS

Marble rolling is a classic kids' art activity that can be used at Halloween time to fashion spiderwebs.

MATERIALS

Scissors
Black or brown paper
Cake pan
Marble(s)
White tempera paint in a small dish
Spoon
White crayon
Black construction paper
Glue

INSTRUCTIONS

1. Cut the paper to fit inside the cake pan.
2. Roll the marble around in the paint dish to cover it with paint. Transfer the marble to the cake pan with the spoon.
3. Tip the pan back and forth several times to send the paint-covered marble around the paper. Recoat the marble with paint as necessary and repeat.
4. Remove the spiderweb painting and let it dry.
5. Draw a spider on black paper with the white crayon and cut it out. Glue it to the spiderweb or glue on a pom-pom spider (page 206).

TAPE-RESIST SKELETON PAINTING

Create spooky life-size skeletons with body tracings and masking tape (two kid favorites) and a coat of black paint.

MATERIALS

Masking tape
White butcher paper or other piece of paper slightly larger than your child's body
Marker
Scissors
Large paintbrush or foam brush
Black paint (tempera or BioColor)

INSTRUCTIONS

1. Tape the corners of the butcher paper to the floor to hold it in place.

2. Have your child lie down on the paper, in any pose desired, and trace her body with a marker. If you'd like to make one yourself, ask your child to trace your body on another sheet of paper.

3. Before creating your skeleton, you may want to learn more (or just get a refresher) about the bones in your body and how they fit together. Look at a picture of a skeleton in a book (we like *See Inside Your Body* by Katie Daynes), study a model of a skeleton (we picked up a small but accurate one from the dollar store for only a few dollars), or just use your fingers and feel where your bones are.

4. Use masking tape to create the bones inside the outline of your paper body. Cut or tear the tape in appropriate lengths for each bone, briefly press the tape to your pants or other clothing (a trick that makes it easier to remove the tape from the paper later), then press the tape bone to the paper where it belongs. Continue with all the bones you want to add. No need to be completely accurate—each of our feet contains 26 bones, after all.

5. Paint over the entire paper, tape and all, with black paint. Let the paint dry completely.
6. Peel the tape skeleton off the paper, piece by piece. Hang the skeleton on the wall, or outside in the dark, for some fun and spooky Halloween decor.

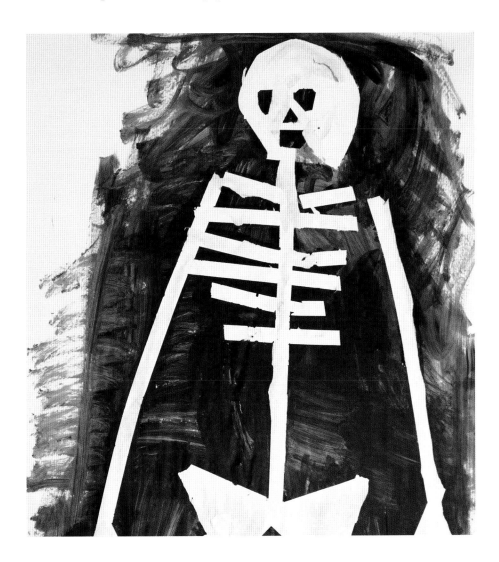

CARDBOARD HAUNTED HOUSE

Children can use their creativity to fashion and decorate a haunted house out of cardboard boxes.

MATERIALS

Cardboard boxes in assorted shapes and sizes, including paper towel rolls, round
    oatmeal or salt boxes, and so on
X-Acto knife (for adult use only) or scissors
Packing tape
Hot glue gun (optional)
Paintbrushes
Tempera or BioColor paints in black, white, brown, orange (or any colors you like)
Tissue paper, fabric, construction paper, or other items for embellishment
    (optional)

INSTRUCTIONS

1. Assemble the basic structure of your haunted house out of the cardboard boxes. You may want just a basic structure (like those pictured here), created out of a single box, with a gabled roof made by taping on the box flaps. Or you may want to assemble a more complex structure out of multiple cardboard boxes, connecting them with a hot glue gun or packing tape.

2. Paint your house with tempera or BioColor paint.

3. Add any additional embellishments as desired. (My older daughter added orange tissue-paper roof tiles and little spiderwebs in the windows.)

Autumn Recipes

Fall is our excuse to bake up a storm, using extra spices and nuts, but especially including pumpkins and apples. Delicious pumpkin is a flavor so unique to autumn that we go a bit crazy with it. We bake pumpkin bars, pumpkin pie, pumpkin–chocolate chip muffins, pumpkin scones, pumpkin waffles, pumpkin rolls, and pumpkin pancakes. In short, nothing is safe from the addition of pumpkin!

Similarly, we look forward to apple picking every year and coming home with bushels of all types. We eat them fresh and make applesauce, apple cake, apple muffins, apple scones, and apple-cheddar hand pies.

APPLE-CHEDDAR HAND PIES

Portable, personal apple pies—how much better can it get than that? These apple hand pies are perfect for autumn picnics, parties, and after-school snacks.

Makes 14–16 hand pies

INGREDIENTS

3 apples
⅓ cup sugar, plus extra for sprinkling
1 teaspoon cinnamon
Pinch of nutmeg
2 teaspoons cornstarch
2 teaspoons lemon juice
Piecrust dough (see page 142)
Flour for rolling the piecrust
2 oz. cheddar cheese, sliced
Egg wash (1 egg whisked with 1 tablespoon water)

INSTRUCTIONS

1. Peel and core the apples and chop them fine.
2. Mix the apples, the $\frac{1}{3}$ cup sugar, spices, cornstarch, and lemon juice in a heavy saucepan. Cook the apples over medium-low heat for 10–15 minutes, until they are softened. Let them cool to warm, not hot.
3. While the apples are cooking, preheat the oven to 375°F and line one or two cookie sheets with baking parchment. Also, bring the piecrust dough out of the fridge to soften slightly (about 15 minutes).
4. Roll out the piecrust dough on a floured surface. Use a 3" round biscuit or cookie cutter to cut rounds out of the dough. Transfer half of the dough rounds to the parchment-lined cookie sheets.
5. Place a small piece of cheese (about 1"–2" square) in the center of each round and top it with a spoonful of apple filling.
6. Cover each pie with a second round of dough (you may want to roll out the top rounds a second time for extra coverage). Press the edges closed with fork tines.
7. Use a sharp knife to cut three or four little air vents in the top crusts. Brush each pie with the egg wash, then sprinkle them with sugar.
8. Bake for 25–35 minutes, or until the crust is golden brown at the edges.
9. Eat the pies warm or at room temperature. Bonus points if you combine your pie with vanilla ice cream or whipped cream.

APPLE BUNDT CAKE

This moist apple cake is filled with wholesome apple goodness.
Makes 2 medium Bundt cakes or 24 muffins

INGREDIENTS

6 cups diced apple (about 5 medium apples)
1½ cups sugar
1 tablespoon cinnamon
½ teaspoon nutmeg, freshly ground
1 cup cinnamon applesauce
1½ sticks (¾ cup) butter, melted and cooled, plus a little to butter the pans
2 teaspoons vanilla
3 eggs
1½ cups white whole wheat flour
1½ cups all-purpose flour, plus a little to sprinkle in the pans
2 teaspoons baking powder
1 teaspoon baking soda
1 teaspoon salt
Powdered sugar or caramel sauce (optional)

INSTRUCTIONS

1. Preheat the oven to 350°F. Butter and flour two medium Bundt pans (about 8" across with 6-cup capacity).
2. Combine the apples, sugar, cinnamon, and nutmeg in a large bowl. Add the applesauce, butter, vanilla, and eggs and mix well. Add the flour, baking powder, baking soda, and salt and stir just until mixed.
3. Pour the batter into the Bundt pans and bake for 40–45 minutes or until a toothpick inserted in the center of the cakes comes out clean.
4. Cool the Bundt cakes for 10 minutes, then invert them on a wire rack. Dust the cakes with powdered sugar or drizzle them with caramel sauce, if desired. This cake is excellent served warm with a scoop of vanilla ice cream.

APPLE MUFFINS

If you're making muffins, line a muffin tin with cupcake papers or silicone muffin liners (or simply grease and flour the muffin tin). Fill each section ⅔ full. Bake for 20–25 minutes or until a toothpick inserted in the center of a muffin comes out clean.

GERMAN APPLE PANCAKES

More of a baked-egg dish than a traditional pancake, but with the addition of delicious caramelized apples, this is my husband's special fall recipe and our family's most requested breakfast during apple season. We usually double it and relish any leftovers we might have. This recipe was adapted from *Baking Illustrated,* by the editors of *Cook's Illustrated* magazine.

Serves 4

INGREDIENTS

2 large eggs
¾ cup half-and-half
1 teaspoon vanilla
½ teaspoon salt
1 tablespoon sugar
½ cup all-purpose flour
6 tablespoons butter
3 Granny Smith apples, peeled and thinly sliced
¼ cup light brown sugar
Powdered sugar, for serving
Maple syrup, for serving
Lemon wedges, for serving

INSTRUCTIONS

1. Preheat the oven to 425°F.
2. Place the first five ingredients in a blender and process until mixed. Add the flour and process again. Set the blender, with the egg-flour mixture, aside.
3. Melt 2 tablespoons of the butter in a heavy-bottom skillet over medium heat. Add the apples and brown sugar and cook, covered, for about 10 minutes or until the apples are soft but still firm, stirring every minute or so.
4. Add the remaining 4 tablespoons of

butter to one large (10–12") or two small (6") heavy, ovenproof pan(s) and put the pan(s) in the preheated oven.

5. When the butter is melted and bubbling but not yet browning, pull out the pan and add the cooked apples. Quickly pour the batter over the apples in the pan and place it in the oven and cook until the pancake is puffy and golden, about 10 minutes.

6. Carefully invert the pancake onto a serving plate. Dust the pancake with powdered sugar and cut it into quarters. Serve it warm with warm maple syrup and a squeeze of lemon.

PUMPKIN WAFFLES

These delicious and healthy waffles are moist and full of pumpkin goodness.

INGREDIENTS

Oil for the waffle iron
¼ cup dark brown sugar
1½ cups white whole wheat flour
2 teaspoons baking powder
½ teaspoon salt
2 teaspoons Pumpkin Pie Spice Mix (page 221)
1 cup canned pumpkin or pumpkin puree
1 cup buttermilk
2 eggs, yolks and whites separated
4 tablespoons butter, melted and cooled
Butter and maple syrup, for serving (optional)
Whipped cream and cinnamon, for serving (optional)

INSTRUCTIONS

1. Oil and preheat the waffle iron. We use a square waffle iron, but you can also use a Belgian waffle maker with this recipe.
2. Mix the dry ingredients in a large bowl.
3. Whisk together the pumpkin, buttermilk, egg yolks, and melted butter in a medium bowl.
4. Add the pumpkin mixture to the dry ingredients and mix until combined.
5. Whip the egg whites until stiff, then fold them into the batter. (This makes the waffles a bit lighter, but if you're pressed for time, you can skip this step and just add the whole egg in step 3).
6. Pour the batter onto your preheated waffle iron and cook.
7. Serve with butter and maple syrup—or with whipped cream and a sprinkle of cinnamon if you want to get fancy.

PUMPKIN PIE SPICE MIX

Pumpkin pie spice is called for in several of the following recipes and is easy to make yourself.

INGREDIENTS

¼ cup cinnamon
2 tablespoons ground ginger
2 teaspoons nutmeg (we use freshly grated, and our seven-year-old daughter loves
    to do the grating)
1 teaspoon ground cloves

INSTRUCTIONS

Simply mix the spices together and store them in an airtight container.

PUMPKIN–CHOCOLATE CHIP MUFFINS

Delicious and moist, these pumpkin–chocolate chip muffins are made healthier with whole wheat flour.

Makes 12 muffins

INGREDIENTS

Butter for greasing muffin pans

1½ cups white whole wheat flour

½ cup sugar, plus extra for sprinkling on top

1 tablespoon baking powder

½ teaspoons salt

1 tablespoon Pumpkin Pie Spice Mix (see page 221)

6 tablespoons cold butter, sliced

1 cup canned pumpkin or pumpkin puree

½ cup buttermilk

1 egg

1½ teaspoons vanilla

½ cup mini chocolate chips

INSTRUCTIONS

1. Preheat the oven to 400°F and grease a 12-count muffin tin (or use liners).

2. Mix the dry ingredients in a food processor.

3. Add the butter to the flour mixture and pulse a few times, or until the butter is pea size or smaller.

4. Transfer the flour-butter mixture to a large bowl.

5. In a separate bowl, mix together the pumpkin, buttermilk, egg, and vanilla.

6. Blend the pumpkin mixture with the flour mixture until the two are just combined.

7. Add the chocolate chips to the batter and fold them in.

8. Spoon the batter into the greased muffin tin in equal amounts for

each cup. (If your kids help with this, as mine do, you might want to reapportion on the sly, as some muffin cups may be overflowing while others are practically empty.)

9. Sprinkle the batter with sugar.

10. Bake the muffins for 20 minutes or until a toothpick inserted in the center of a muffin comes out clean. Cool the muffins in the pan slightly, then enjoy. They're delicious warm or at room temperature.

PUMPKIN JACK-O'-LANTERN PANCAKES

Pumpkin pancakes are a lovely way to start a fall weekend. Add faces to make these extra fun for kids.

INGREDIENTS

1½ cups white whole wheat flour

2 tablespoons sugar

1½ teaspoons baking powder

¼ teaspoon salt

2 teaspoons Pumpkin Pie Spice Mix (see page 221)

1½ cups whole milk

¾ cup canned pumpkin or pumpkin puree

2 eggs

2 tablespoons melted butter, cooled

1 banana (raisins or chocolate chips work well, too, but they don't produce the glowing yellow eyes of the cooked banana)

Butter or vegetable oil for greasing the griddle

Butter and maple syrup, for serving

INSTRUCTIONS

1. Preheat the griddle or pan.
2. Whisk the dry ingredients together in a large bowl.
3. Mix the milk, pumpkin, egg, and melted butter.
4. Pour the pumpkin mix into the dry ingredients and stir until they're just combined.
5. Slice the banana into coins. Cut some into thirds (for triangles) and some in half.
6. Grease the griddle.
7. Use a small pitcher or a measuring cup with a pour spout to pour pumpkin-shaped pancakes on the griddle. You may need to use the back of a spoon to help spread the pancake mix into shape.

8. Add the banana coins and triangles to form the jack-o'-lantern face.

9. When the edges of the pancake start drying out and bubbles start forming, flip the pancakes over to continue cooking on the other side.

10. Remove the pancakes from the griddle and serve them with butter and maple syrup. The banana jack-o'-lantern features really glow once the butter and syrup are added.

PUMPKIN ROLLS

These soft pumpkin rolls make great little turkey sandwiches if you have leftovers after Thanksgiving.

INGREDIENTS

1 cup milk
¼ cup water
⅓ cup brown sugar
1 teaspoon salt
1 tablespoon Pumpkin Pie Spice Mix (see page 221)
2 eggs
4 teaspoons active dry yeast
2½ cups white whole wheat flour
2½ cups all-purpose flour, plus extra for rolling if needed
½ cup (1 stick) butter
1 cup canned pumpkin or pumpkin puree

INSTRUCTIONS

1. Whisk milk, water, brown sugar, salt, and pumpkin pie spice together in a saucepan. Heat the mixture over low heat until warm (not hot).

2. Remove the pan from the heat and mix in the eggs and yeast.

3. Mix the flours together in a large bowl. Make a well in the center and pour in the milk-egg mixture (but don't stir). Cover the bowl with a lid or plate and set aside for 30 minutes.

4. Meanwhile, melt the butter in a small pan. Remove from heat. Add the pumpkin puree and stir until blended.

5. When the 30 minutes are up, add the pumpkin-butter mixture to the bowl of flour and stir to combine the ingredients.

6. Place the dough on a clean counter and shape it into a ball. Cover the dough with the inverted bowl and let it rise for 20 minutes.

7. Knead the dough lightly on a floured surface, then shape it into small rolls. The dough is sticky, but try not to add too much flour. (I flatten the dough into a rectangle, use a sharp knife to cut it into squares, then roll each into a ball with the help of a little flour.) Place the rolls on a parchment-lined cookie sheet. Let them rise for another 20 minutes.

8. During this last rise, preheat the oven to 400°F.

9. Bake the rolls for 15 minutes. They are delicious warm or at room temperature.

PUMPKIN-PECAN SCONES WITH CREAM CHEESE SPREAD

These scones are delicious on a fall morning. For those who don't care for nuts, dried cranberries are an excellent substitute.

Makes 8 large or 12 small scones

INGREDIENTS

For the Scones

1 cup white whole wheat flour
1 cup all-purpose flour
½ cup brown sugar
1 tablespoon baking powder
½ teaspoon salt
1 tablespoon Pumpkin Pie Spice Mix (page 221)
½ cup (1 stick) butter, cold and sliced
½ cup canned pumpkin or pumpkin puree
½ cup cream or half-and-half
1 cup pecans (candied pecans are especially luscious in these scones), whole or in pieces
Cinnamon sugar, for sprinkling (1 tablespoon sugar mixed with ½ teaspoon cinnamon)

For the Cream Cheese Spread

½ cup whipped cream cheese
½ cup powdered sugar or 2 tablespoons honey

INSTRUCTIONS

1. Preheat the oven to 400°F. Line a cookie sheet with baking parchment.
2. Measure all the dry ingredients into a food processor. Run for a minute to mix.
3. Add the butter slices to the flour mixture. Pulse several times until

the butter is pea size or smaller. Or you can just mix the dry ingredients and then cut in the butter using a pastry blender or knife and fork.

4. Transfer the flour mixture to a large bowl.

5. In a medium bowl, whisk together the pumpkin and cream.

6. Add the pumpkin mixture to the flour mixture. Mix until combined. Fold in the pecans.

7. Turn the dough out onto the counter. Knead just a bit to shape the dough into a round about 1" thick and cut it into eight wedges. If you prefer smaller scones, shape the dough into two equal rounds before cutting each into six wedges and reduce the cooking time by a few minutes. Sprinkle each scone with cinnamon sugar.

8. Bake the scones for 20 minutes. Let them cool on the pan for 10 minutes.

9. Mix the ingredients for the cream cheese spread together. Break off a scone piece and spread it with the cream cheese mixture or cut the scone in half horizontally before spreading it with the cream cheese. Enjoy!

PUMPKIN BARS WITH GINGERSNAP CRUST

These bars, with their gingersnap crust topped by a luscious layer of pumpkin pie, are a perfect combination of fall flavors.

Makes about 30 bars

INGREDIENTS

1 package gingersnap cookies (about 14 oz.)
6 tablespoons butter, melted
8 oz. cream cheese, softened
¾ cup brown sugar
1¼ cups canned pumpkin
2 eggs
1 tablespoon Pumpkin Pie Spice Mix (see page 221)
1 teaspoon vanilla
½ teaspoon salt

INSTRUCTIONS

1. Preheat the oven to 350°F. Line a 9" x 13" pan with baking parchment.
2. Place the gingersnap cookies in a food processor and process them into crumbs. Add the melted butter and pulse to mix.
3. Press the gingersnap mixture evenly into the bottom of the pan. Bake for 10 minutes.
4. To make the filling, mix the cream cheese and brown sugar in a bowl with an electric beater. Add the pumpkin and mix until they're combined. Add the eggs, pumpkin pie spice, vanilla, and salt and mix them thoroughly, scraping down the sides of the bowl with a rubber spatula.
5. Pour the filling over the crust and bake for 30 minutes or until the filling is firm.
6. Let the pan cool on a wire rack, then lift the bars out of the pan by holding two sides of the baking parchment. Cut the bars into squares and serve. To store, keep the bars covered in the refrigerator.

Thanksgiving

Autumn wraps up nicely with families sharing Thanksgiving together. We enjoy a feast of harvest foods and give thanks for the people and blessings in our lives. Turkeys and pilgrims fill our imaginations now, with schoolchildren the nation over creating hand turkeys and reenacting the Pilgrims' first Thanksgiving.

OUR FAVORITE BOOKS ABOUT THANKSGIVING

Over the River and through the Wood by Lydia Maria Child
Cranberry Thanksgiving by Wende and Harry Devlin
I Know an Old Lady Who Swallowed a Pie by Alison Jackson
Thanks for Thanksgiving by Julie Markes
10 Fat Turkeys by Tony Johnston
Thanksgiving Is for Giving Thanks by Margaret Sutherland

THANKFUL STONES

Combining a favorite artful activity (melted-crayon rocks) with a thankfulness activity makes these stones perfect for the season.

MATERIALS

Black Sharpie
Melted-Crayon Rocks, page 42

INSTRUCTIONS

1. Using the Sharpie, write words on the melted-crayon stones that represent what you are thankful for. Children can write their own words, draw pictures, or dictate words for you to write.

2. Gather the thankful stones in a basket, perhaps in the center of your dining table. You can use them to talk about the things you are thankful for or just keep them as a reminder.

THANKSGIVING LEAF BANNER

String autumn leaves together for this seasonal banner, adding words and images with metallic Sharpies.

MATERIALS

Metallic Sharpies
Dried and pressed leaves (see page 176)
Newspaper or plastic place mat
½" wide ribbon, in length desired
Hot glue gun

INSTRUCTIONS

1. Draw or write things you are thankful for on your leaves.
2. Protect your work surface with newspaper or an art mat (such as a cheap plastic place mat). Lay your ribbon facedown along the work surface.
3. Arrange your leaves in the order desired along the length of the ribbon, facedown.
4. Using the hot glue gun, glue each leaf stem to the ribbon, one at a time.
5. Hang the banner on the wall or in the window for a beautiful and unique autumn decoration.

VARIATION

Instead of making a banner with your leaves, use string to tie the leaves to bare branches stuck in a pot of sand. (Thanks to my friend Kari Richmond for this idea.)

NOT-A-HAND TURKEY

This is simply an exercise to encourage children (and parents) who may be accustomed to using a hand tracing or handprint to form their turkeys to try different ways of drawing them.

MATERIALS

Pictures of turkeys
Drawing tools (such as markers or crayons)
Paper

INSTRUCTIONS

1. Start by looking at turkeys together, either real ones (at a farm or zoo) or pictures of them (in books or on the Internet). Talk about what the turkey looks like—the body, the tail feathers, the long neck, the colors, the wattle.

2. Provide drawing materials so your child can draw a turkey, using the images and ideas she has just assimilated. If your child wants help, you can talk about the main shapes that form the turkey body while she draws.

3. Encourage her to draw different kinds of turkeys or draw a turkey from different angles each time by asking "How would you draw a turkey from the front?" or "What would that turkey look like from the back?" (Or running, or sleeping, and so on.) The point is not to get her to draw a perfect turkey (there's no such thing anyway) but to get her to think beyond the hand turkey and to inspire her to try different ways to depict something that she may be used to drawing the same way each time.

LEAF-PRINT CLOTH NAPKINS

Enjoy the beauty of nature at the dinner table with these leaf-print napkins.

MATERIALS

Newspaper or a splat mat and scrap paper

Spoon

Fabric paint (I like the Jacquard brand.)

Large plate or acrylic box frame, for rolling out the ink

Mini paint roller (from the hardware store, used for corners and trim in house painting)

Leaves and ferns

Plain white or light-colored cloth napkins, or make your own (see the Picnic Napkins on page 122)

Brayer (hard rubber roller, found at arts and crafts supply stores) or rolling pin

Iron

Ironing board

INSTRUCTIONS

1. Prepare for leaf printing by protecting your work surface with newspaper or a splat mat. Gather all of your materials.

2. Put a couple spoonfuls of fabric paint on the plate. Roll it around with the paint roller to coat the roller thinly.

3. Place a leaf, vein side up, on a sheet of newspaper or scrap paper. Roll the paint roller over the leaf to coat it evenly.

4. Set the leaf, paint side down, on the napkin where you want the print. Set a clean piece of paper over the leaf. Roll the brayer over the paper-covered leaf to press it down evenly. Carefully lift up the paper and leaf to reveal your print.

5. Continue with the rest of your napkins.

6. Let the napkins dry overnight, and then iron them, following the instructions on the fabric paint bottle to set the paint.

WINTER

Winter is the time for comfort, for good food and warmth, for the touch of a friendly hand and for a talk beside the fire: it is the time for home.

—EDITH SITWELL

WINTER PROJECTS

CELEBRATING WINTER

WINTER HOLIDAYS, crafts, and decorations are my favorites, and they help me get through what is admittedly the bleakest part of the year for me. The dark, cold days of winter are made fun and bright with candlelight, fires in the hearth, holiday baking and decorating, extra family time, and a succession of festive holidays.

Winter and the holiday season officially start for us each year when we drive to the Christmas tree farm after Thanksgiving to choose our tree. We strap the year's perfect tree on top of the car, drive home, and take the box of ornaments and decorations out of storage. From then on, it's a month of holiday decorating, baking, crafting, shopping, and parties.

As much as we love the holidays, afterward, of course, we are ready to slow down and simplify, focusing more on building snowmen (when we *have* snow, which is less frequent in North Carolina than my kids would like), reading, playing games, and doing quiet arts and crafts activities. And then around comes Valentine's Day, just when we are ready for another fun holiday to celebrate.

Christmas

Christmas is my favorite holiday, the one with twinkling lights, a little extra baking and crafting, and perhaps best of all, the excitement and wonder of children. We drape the house with strings of lights and candles to brighten dark mornings and evenings, and we love to drive around town to admire the glowing windows and outdoor holiday displays of other homes.

We decorate our house using a combination of the old and the new: old ornaments stored away in our Christmas box complemented by whatever we create that year. Our decor is always added to, bit by bit, over the season. We make paper chains, snowflakes, salt-dough ornaments, garlands, and stained glass. We draw and paint and collage.

OUR FAVORITE BOOKS ABOUT CHRISTMAS

The Little Drummer Boy by Ezra Jack Keats
The Night before Christmas by Clement C. Moore
Room for a Little One: A Christmas Tale by Martin Waddell
A Wish to Be a Christmas Tree by Colleen Monroe
The Polar Express by Chris Van Allsburg
The Spirit of Christmas by Nancy Tillman

AN ADVENT CALENDAR CHAIN

This activity-based Advent calendar is relatively easy to make and use. Get the kids involved or make it on your own and surprise them.

MATERIALS

Paper cut into 24 different-size circles
Sewing machine
Scissors
Potato-printed stars or other shapes (see page 31)
White glue, such as Elmer's
List of 24 Advent activity ideas (see below)

INSTRUCTIONS

1. Sew the paper circles into one long chain with a continuous, simple basting stitch down the center of the chain, with little to no space between each circle.

2. Cut out your potato-print shapes and glue one to the center of each paper circle. Write or stamp the numbers 1 through 24, one on each shape. Let them dry.

3. Hang your chain vertically on the first day of Advent, with number 24 at the top and number 1 at the bottom.

4. Each day you can either snip off that day's circle or pull off the star or other shape from the circle. Refer to the corresponding Advent activity list (keep it handy— perhaps taped inside a cupboard door) to find the activity for the day. Or simply write the activity on the back of the circle.

ADVENT ACTIVITY IDEAS

Make snowflake Christmas cards.

Decorate salt-dough ornaments.

Head to the library to pick out some Christmas books.

Drive to a Christmas tree farm to choose a tree.

String cranberries and popcorn to decorate the tree.

Make paper chains.

Invite a friend over to paint finger- or toenails red and green.

Make an ice wreath.

Make a gingerbread house.

Decorate gingerbread men.

Make pinecone ornaments for the birds and hang them outside.

Make candied and spiced nuts.

Have a family art night and make a holiday mural together.

Wrap gifts.

Create snowflake window decorations.

Make a batch of candy cane playdough.

Go for a winter nature hike.

Play games and drink hot chocolate.

Bake Christmas cookies.

Invite a friend over to decorate cookies.

Make popcorn and watch a Christmas movie together.

Go for a drive to look at Christmas lights.

Sing carols.

Build a snowman.

MAKING SALT DOUGH

Salt dough is easily and inexpensively made with basic kitchen ingredients. When mixing the dough, you can even add cinnamon for lovely scented ornaments or food coloring for dyed dough.

INGREDIENTS

4 cups all-purpose flour
1 cup salt
1½ cups cold water

INSTRUCTIONS

1. Mix the flour and salt together in a large bowl. Add the water and stir. If necessary, add up to another ½ cup of water, a little at a time, until the dough pulls together.
2. Store the dough in a plastic freezer bag in the fridge until ready to use.

BASIC SALT-DOUGH ORNAMENTS

Salt dough can be shaped with cookie cutters and baked hard, making it popular for holiday ornaments.

MATERIALS

1 batch Salt Dough (see page 245)
Rolling pin
Baking parchment
Cookie cutters
Plastic drinking straws
Cookie sheet
Paint, such as BioColor, activity paint, or tempera paint (optional)
Paintbrush (optional)
Glitter (optional)
Thin jewelry wire or ribbon, for hanging (or use ornament hooks)

INSTRUCTIONS

1. Tear off a fist-size section of salt dough and roll it out on a sheet of baking parchment to about a ¼" thick.

2. Use cookie cutters to cut out shapes. Pull away the extra dough from around the cookie cutter shapes.

3. Use a plastic drinking straw to punch a hanging hole at the top of each ornament.

4. Transfer the baking paper with the salt-dough ornaments to a cookie sheet. Bake the ornaments at 250°F for 2–3 hours or until they're hard. Let them cool.

5. Paint the ornaments with BioColor or other paints, adding glitter to the wet paint if desired (optional).

6. Thread the jewelry wire through the hole and twist the ends to form a loop. Hang the ornaments on the tree or elsewhere.

BEADED SALT-DOUGH ORNAMENTS

Small glass beads can be pressed into and baked in the salt-dough ornaments to create a beautiful stained glass effect.

MATERIALS

Basic Salt-Dough Ornaments (see page 246), uncooked
Small glass beads

INSTRUCTIONS

1. Press small glass beads into the uncooked salt-dough ornaments. You can use the beads to create specific designs, or you can place them in an all-over random pattern.

2. Follow steps 3–6 for Basic Salt-Dough Ornaments to finish.

STAMPED SALT-DOUGH ORNAMENTS

Salt dough readily accepts rubber stamps, which create attractive designs on the surface of the ornament.

MATERIALS

Basic Salt-Dough Ornaments (see page 246), uncooked
Rubber stamps
Ink pads
Paint, such as BioColor (optional)

INSTRUCTIONS

1. Use the rubber stamps and stamp pad ink to stamp designs into the uncooked salt-dough ornaments. Press firmly but not too deeply.
2. Follow steps 3–4 for Basic Salt-Dough Ornaments.
3. If desired, paint the cooked ornaments, as in step 5 for Basic Salt-Dough Ornaments. The stamped design should remain, if it was pressed in firmly, although the stamp ink will be covered up.
4. Follow step 6 to finish.

STAINED GLASS SALT-DOUGH ORNAMENTS

In these ornaments, the salt dough forms the frame, and the center is filled with glue (which dries somewhat transparent) and colorful, translucent beads.

MATERIALS

Basic Salt-Dough Ornaments (see page 246), uncooked
Small cookie cutters (or a sharp knife) to cut designs out of the center of the
    ornaments
Cookie sheet
Plastic wrap
White glue, such as Elmer's
Tempera paint (optional)
Translucent pony beads or glass beads
Glitter, sequins, colored tissue paper (optional)

INSTRUCTIONS

1. Use the small cookie cutters or sharp knife to cut the centers out of the salt-dough ornaments.
2. Follow steps 3–5 for the Basic Salt-Dough Ornaments.
3. Place the cooked salt-dough ornaments on a cookie sheet covered with plastic wrap. Fill the center of each ornament with the white glue. If you like, color the glue first with some tempera paint.
4. Set the beads in the wet glue. Alternatively, sprinkle the glue with glitter or sequins, or add colored tissue paper. Let the glue dry completely (about 2–3 days).
5. Follow step 6 for the Basic Salt-Dough Ornaments to finish.
6. Hang the ornaments on the Christmas tree or in the window and admire them with the light shining through.

LACY SALT-DOUGH ORNAMENTS

Punch holes in your salt dough to create these elegant, lacelike ornaments.

MATERIALS

Basic Salt-Dough Ornaments (see page 246), uncooked
Scissors
Plastic drinking straws

INSTRUCTIONS

1. Cut the drinking straws into thirds (they get gunked up with the salt dough and you'll want a bunch).
2. Punch the end of the straw into the salt-dough ornament and pull it back out, creating a hole in the ornament. Continue to punch as many holes as desired. You can create specific designs or an all-over pattern.
3. Follow steps 4–6 for the Basic Salt-Dough Ornaments to finish.

SALT-DOUGH GINGERBREAD HOUSE LANTERN

This lantern is magical, much loved in our house, and definitely worth the extra effort to make.

MATERIALS

1 batch of Salt Dough (see page 245)
Rolling pin
Baking parchment
Tiny gingerbread house template (see page 331)
Table knife (for kids), or sharp knife (for adults)
Glass beads
Straw (optional)
Cookie sheet
Scissors (optional)
Foam brush or regular paintbrush
Mod Podge
Hot glue gun
Candle in a glass votive holder

INSTRUCTIONS

1. Divide the salt dough into four or five sections and roll each one out separately on a sheet of parchment to about a ¼" thick.

2. Set the gingerbread house template pieces on top of each rolled-out salt-dough section. Use a knife to cut out the salt dough in the shape of the template. Pull the extra dough away from the house sections.

3. Decorate the house pieces by pressing glass beads into the salt dough. You can also use a straw to punch a lacy design if desired.

4. Transfer each sheet of baking parchment with its house section to a cookie sheet. You can trim the parchment paper around the salt dough in order to fit more pieces on a cookie sheet at one time.

5. Bake the gingerbread house pieces at 250°F for 2–4 hours, until hard. Let the pieces cool.

6. Brush the salt dough with Mod Podge for shine and protection (this also helps tiny glass beads to stick to the salt dough). Let the pieces dry.

7. Assemble the salt-dough gingerbread house, using a hot glue gun to hold the sections together.

8. Light a candle in a glass votive holder under the gingerbread house and admire it in the dark.

SHRINKY DINKS ORNAMENTS

Children love to watch their drawings shrink before their eyes, becoming miniature ornaments, perfect for a doll tree (page 255).

MATERIALS

Permanent markers, such as Sharpies
Shrinky Dink plastic
Scissors
Hole punch
Cookie sheet
Thread or embroidery floss

INSTRUCTIONS

1. With a permanent marker, draw and color in images for your ornaments directly on the Shrinky Dink plastic, making them about twice as large as you want the finished ornament to be.
2. Cut out the ornaments. Punch a hole in the top for hanging them.
3. Spread the ornaments out on a cookie sheet. Bake at 325°F until the ornaments shrink and flatten out, which can take up to 10 minutes. (*Note:* First they curl up as part of the shrinking process, but then they flatten out.) Children will enjoy watching this through the oven door window.
4. Let the ornaments cool.
5. Hang the ornaments on a tabletop or other small Christmas tree (see next activity) using thread or embroidery floss.

A CHRISTMAS TREE FOR THE DOLLS

If your kids are like mine, they love anything miniature, and decorating a tree for their doll and animal friends creates another layer of enchantment for a holiday filled with magic.

MATERIALS

Tabletop-size Christmas tree, such as a small potted tree, the top off a larger Christmas tree, or simply some pine boughs in a vase
A small string of miniature Christmas lights
Miniature ornaments, such as Shrinky Dinks Ornaments (see page 254), small salt-dough ornaments (see page 246), jingle bells, large buttons, a string of beads
Gifts for dolls and animals (optional)

INSTRUCTIONS

1. Trim the miniature tree with the minilights and ornaments.
2. Place small boxes or little handmade gifts for the dolls and stuffed animals under the tree if desired.

TISSUE-PAPER STAINED GLASS BUNTING

Decorate for the season with a bunting that will shine in both sunlight and holiday lights.

MATERIALS

Scissors
Colored tissue paper in Christmas colors
Transparent contact paper (also called sticky-back plastic)
Clear tape, such as Scotch tape
Hot glue gun (optional)
¼" wide ribbon (optional)

INSTRUCTIONS

1. Cut the colored tissue paper into stars, triangles, squares, or random shapes.
2. Cut off a section of contact paper about 6" wide. Tape it to the table, paper side up. Pull off the paper backing.
3. Press the colored-tissue-paper shapes to the contact paper, covering most of it. Cover the tissue-paper design with another sheet of contact paper.
4. Cut the tissue-paper stained glass into triangles.
5. To create the bunting, either run clear tape along the top of the triangles to connect them (folding it over itself and the triangles) or use the hot glue gun and the ribbon.
6. Hang the bunting in the window where the sun will shine through it.

TISSUE-PAPER STAINED GLASS PAPER CHAIN

As with the Tissue-Paper Stained Glass Bunting, this paper chain glows both in sunlight and at night with Christmas lights.

MATERIALS

Scissors
Colored tissue paper
Transparent contact paper (also called sticky-back plastic)
Clear tape

INSTRUCTIONS

1. Follow steps 1–3 for the Tissue-Paper Stained Glass Bunting (see page 256).
2. Cut the tissue-paper stained glass into 1" wide strips.
3. Tape one of the strips end to end (overlapping by about ½"–1") to form a loop. Insert another strip into the first and tape it end to end to form another loop. Continue to form loop after loop to create a paper chain as long as desired.
4. Hang the stained glass paper chain on the Christmas tree or in the window.

COLORED-FILM PAPER CHAIN

This colorful paper chain is quickly and easily assembled from a simple pack of index dividers.

MATERIALS

Scissors
Index dividers (file-folder size) made out of translucent colored film
Stapler

INSTRUCTIONS

1. Cut the index dividers into 1" wide strips.
2. Staple one of the strips end to end (overlapping by about ½"–1") to form a loop. Insert another strip into the first and staple it end to end to form another loop. Continue to form loop after loop, to create a paper chain as long as desired.
3. Hang the colored-film paper chain on the Christmas tree or in the window.

CANDY CANE PLAYDOUGH GIFTS

Candy cane playdough makes a great gift to give all the young kids in your life.

Makes about 1 dozen mason jar gifts

MATERIALS

1 batch candy cane playdough (see page 18)
Knife
Twelve 1-pint mason jars with lids
Scissors
Yarn
Hole punch
Labels (see template on page 332)
Christmasy fabric, cut into squares or circles about 5" in diameter

INSTRUCTIONS

1. Cut each of the playdough colors into about twelve sections.
2. Roll each section out into a snake. Twist a white snake and a red snake together to make a candy cane.
3. Fit the candy cane into a mason jar. Add the circle part of the lid.
4. Cut the yarn into 4" pieces and loop the yarn through a hole punched in each label. To make a more decorative gift, set the yarn ends of the label over the lid and then place the fabric square on top. Screw on the rim of the lid to hold everything in place.

COFFEE FILTER CHRISTMAS BUNTING

Coffee filters are fun to paint with liquid watercolors and look quite festive when strung together as a bunting.

MATERIALS

White coffee filters (the bowl-shaped kind rather than the cone shape)
Liquid watercolors in Christmas colors
Paintbrushes and/or droppers
¼" wide ribbon
Glue stick

INSTRUCTIONS

1. Paint the coffee filters with liquid watercolors using paintbrushes or droppers. Let the filters dry.
2. To make the bunting, fold a painted coffee filter in half over the ribbon and glue the two ends together.
3. Continue adding the rest of the painted coffee filters, spacing them as desired.
4. Hang the bunting on the wall, over the mantel, or on the Christmas tree.

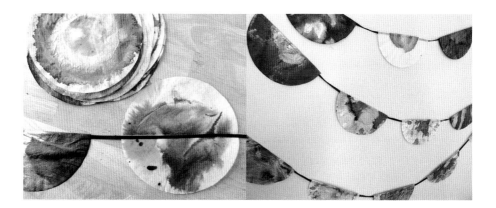

STYROFOAM-PRINTED HOLIDAY CARDS

Styrofoam printing is a childhood classic for a reason. Kids can easily draw holiday images into the Styrofoam, then transfer them to cards in any colors they desire.

MATERIALS

Scissors
Flat Styrofoam, perhaps from a grocery store Styrofoam tray
Thin copy paper
Pen
Newspaper or splat mat to protect workspace
Water-based printing ink
Acrylic box frame or a flat-bottomed baking dish
Brayer (hard rubber roller)
Spoon
A set of plain (blank) note cards and envelopes

INSTRUCTIONS

1. Cut the Styrofoam to the size of the card print you would like to make. Cut the copy paper to the same size.

2. Draw an image on the thin copy paper with the pen.

3. Place the drawing over the Styrofoam and draw over the image again, pressing down evenly but firmly to create an incised drawing on the Styrofoam (the pointy end of a thin paintbrush works well, too, and is less likely to break through the paper). Remove the paper.

4. Protect your workspace with newspaper or a splat mat and assemble all of your printmaking materials.

5. Squirt a bit of the printing ink on the acrylic frame and roll your brayer over it to coat it thinly and evenly.

6. Roll the ink-covered brayer over the Styrofoam that now has an impression of your drawing.

7. Place a blank note card over the Styrofoam. Rub all over the note

card evenly and firmly with the back of the spoon to transfer the inked image to the paper.

8. Repeat the inking and printing process with any number of note cards.

9. Let the cards dry overnight, then add your message to the interior of the cards. If desired, add a note on the back of the card about the name of the artist and the date of the artwork. Slip the cards into envelopes to mail to friends and family.

3-D STAINED GLASS WREATH

If you have a Bundt pan, it's probably in need of an extra job now and again. Let it be the mold for this colorful stained glass wreath in between baking Bundt cakes.

MATERIALS

Bundt pan
Plastic wrap
Cookie sheet
White glue, such as Elmer's
Water
Foam brush or paintbrush
Tissue paper, both light and bright colors
Scissors
Hole punch
Narrow ribbon
Wide ribbon (optional)
Christmas lights (optional)

INSTRUCTIONS

1. Wrap the outside of a Bundt pan tightly and completely with plastic wrap. Cover the cookie sheet (or other work surface) with plastic wrap as well.
2. Set the Bundt pan on the cookie sheet, rounded side up.
3. Thin the glue with water (about 1 part water to 2 parts glue). Brush the plastic-covered Bundt pan all over with the glue mixture. Lay light-colored tissue paper over the pan pressing it against the Bundt form. Brush more glue over the tissue paper. Repeat with another layer of light-colored tissue paper and another layer of glue.
4. Cut the bright-colored tissue paper into stars or other shapes. Press the stars to the light-colored tissue paper and brush more glue over the stars. Let everything dry.

5. Turn the Bundt pan over, cut the plastic, and gently pull the wreath (with plastic) off the pan. The wreath will hold its shape now, like papier-mâché.

6. Trim the edges of the wreath to remove excess plastic wrap and to make the edge even. Trim the inside to create a hole in the center of the wreath.

7. Punch a hole through the tissue paper near the edge of the wreath.

Loop a thin ribbon through the hole and tie the ends together for hanging the wreath. You can also decorate the wreath with a larger ribbon tied in a bow if desired.

8. Hang the wreath in the window to admire in the sunlight, or loop a small string of white Christmas lights around the inside of the wreath form (I held mine in oh-so-professionally with a paper plate and tape), for a lighted nighttime wreath.

Winter and Holiday Food

Winter is our excuse to bake, bake, bake. We keep our kitchen and home cozy and fragrant with a combination of holiday treats, warming soups, and nourishing whole-grain bread. We indulge our sweet tooth with cookies, cakes, and candies— some for ourselves, some as gifts for family and friends.

CRANBERRY-ORANGE CAKES

Jewel-like mini cranberry cakes are made in a muffin tin and will add a festive splash of color to the end of any holiday meal.

INGREDIENTS

¾ cup butter, softened, plus a little extra to melt for greasing the muffin tin
1 cup sugar
1 teaspoon orange zest
2 cups fresh cranberries
1 egg
1 teaspoon vanilla
½ cup orange juice
½ cup plain or vanilla yogurt
1 cup all-purpose flour
1 teaspoon baking powder
½ teaspoon salt
Whipped cream or vanilla ice cream, for serving (optional)

INSTRUCTIONS

1. Preheat the oven to 375°F. Grease a large 12-section muffin tin (I let my daughter use a pastry brush and melted butter for this step—her favorite).

2. Melt ¼ cup of the butter in a cast-

iron pan on the stove top over medium heat. Mix in ½ cup of the sugar, the orange zest, and the cranberries. Divide the mixture evenly among the 12 muffin cups, making sure to include all of the butter-sugar mixture along with the cranberries.

3. Cream the remaining ½ cup butter and ½ cup sugar in a medium bowl with an electric mixer. Add the egg, vanilla, orange juice, and yogurt and beat until well combined. Finally, mix in the flour, baking powder, and salt. Spoon the cake

batter over the cranberries, again dividing it equally among the cups.

4. Bake the cakes for 25 minutes or until the very edges look golden brown and a little crispy. Remove the muffin tin from the oven and let it cool for 5 minutes. Holding a large cooling rack securely over the top of the muffin tin, turn them both over, inverting the cranberry cakes onto the rack.

5. Eat the cakes warm or at room temperature. They're especially good with a dollop of whipped cream or a scoop of vanilla ice cream.

CHERRY-ALMOND SCONES

This is my all-time favorite scone. I usually freeze a batch of uncooked scones, then bake just a few at a time. They can go straight from the freezer to a preheated oven. (I add 1–2 minutes to the cooking time.)

Makes 12 scones

INGREDIENTS

1 cup white whole wheat flour
1 cup all-purpose flour
¼ cup sugar, plus extra for sprinkling on top
2 teaspoons baking powder
½ teaspoon baking soda
½ teaspoon salt
2 teaspoons lemon zest
6 tablespoons cold butter, sliced
¾ cup dried sour cherries, roughly chopped
¾ cup sliced almonds
½ cup cream, plus extra for brushing on top (I sometimes use buttermilk.)
1 egg, beaten
¼ teaspoon almond extract

INSTRUCTIONS

1. Preheat the oven to 425°F. Line a cookie sheet with baking parchment.
2. Measure all the dry ingredients (including the lemon zest) into a food processor. Run it for a minute to mix them.
3. Add the butter pieces to the flour mixture. Pulse the food processor several times until the butter is pea size or smaller. (Or you can just mix the dry ingredients and then cut in the butter using a pastry blender or knife and fork.)
4. Transfer the flour mixture to a large bowl and mix in the dried cherries and sliced almonds.

5. Make a well in the center of the flour mixture and pour in the ½ cup cream, egg, and almond extract. Mix the ingredients until they are combined and the dough starts to come together.

6. Turn the dough out onto the counter and shape it into two rounds. Cut each round, like a pie, into six wedges.

7. Brush the tops of the scones with cream and sprinkle sugar on top.

8. Bake for 15 minutes. Let the scones cool slightly. Yum!

GRANDMA'S CANDY CANE COOKIES

Enjoy these festive cookies with a glass of milk, give them as gifts, or leave a plate out for Santa on Christmas Eve. This recipe has been passed down to me by my grandma and is well remembered by my mom from her childhood. Children love to roll out the cookie-dough snakes and twist them into candy cane shapes.

INGREDIENTS

1 cup butter, softened
1 cup powdered sugar
1 egg
1½ teaspoons almond extract
1 teaspoon vanilla
2½ cups all-purpose flour, plus extra for rolling the dough
1 teaspoon salt
½ teaspoon red food coloring (If you want a natural alternative, try the India Tree brand.)

INSTRUCTIONS

1. Preheat the oven to 375°F. Mix together the butter, sugar, egg, almond extract, and vanilla with an electric mixer. Sift in the flour and salt.

2. Divide the dough evenly, removing half and wrapping it in plastic wrap (shape it into a flattened ball as you do so). Blend red food coloring into the remaining half, then wrap this dough in plastic as well. Place both dough balls in the fridge for an hour, or until firm.

3. Working on a floured surface, roll the dough into thin snakes about 4" long, then twist the two colors together. (*Note:* Younger children may have difficulty twisting the two colors together. My three-year-old enjoyed making a candy cane shape out of one color and pressing bits of the other color along it for the stripes.) Place the twisted dough on a parchment-lined cookie sheet and curve the top down to make

a candy cane shape. Repeat with the remaining dough. Sprinkle the candy canes with sugar for a little extra sparkle.

4. Bake the cookies for 9 minutes. Remove them from the oven and let them cool on the cookie sheet for 5 minutes. Transfer the cookies to a cooling rack and let them cool completely. The cookies are somewhat fragile, so handle them carefully.

CHOCOLATE-DIPPED PRETZELS

Pretzels dipped in melted chocolate are a supereasy and fun holiday treat that even the youngest kids can make.

INGREDIENTS

Chocolate chips
Pretzels
Colored sprinkles

INSTRUCTIONS

1. Melt the chocolate chips in a double boiler or in the microwave.
2. Dip the pretzels in the melted chocolate, then set them on a parchment-lined cookie sheet.

Decorate them with colored sprinkles, then let the chocolate cool and harden.
3. Eat the pretzels or give them as a gift.

TROPICAL CROCK-POT OATMEAL

Have a hot, healthy breakfast ready when you wake up. This tropical version of oatmeal will help you escape to paradise for a few minutes when it's still snowy outside.

INGREDIENTS

1 cup steel cut oats (you can use old-fashioned rolled oats, too, but double the amount of oats if you do)

2½ cups water

1 15 oz. can coconut milk

½ teaspoon vanilla

1 teaspoon cinnamon

¼ teaspoon cardamom (optional)

½–1 cup dried tropical fruit, such as mango, chopped (optional)

Toppings such as fresh tropical fruit (banana, mango, pineapple, papaya), honey, shredded coconut, and/or nuts

Milk

INSTRUCTIONS

1. Mix all the ingredients except the toppings and milk in your Crock-Pot or slow cooker. Cook on low for 6–8 hours.
2. Serve with the desired toppings and milk.

STOVE-TOP VERSION

This works too: Bring the water to a boil and add the oats. Stir in the remaining ingredients, except the toppings and milk, and simmer uncovered for approximately 40 minutes, until the oats are soft and the liquid has been absorbed.

TINY GINGERBREAD HOUSE

Every child wants to make a gingerbread house at Christmas. This miniature version is easily decorated by a child (parents may want to assemble it for younger children) and is small enough to eat. These houses are great for a family creation or as a children's holiday party activity.

INGREDIENTS

Gingerbread cookie dough (use your favorite recipe)
Flour for rolling the dough
Tiny gingerbread house template (see page 331), or make your own
Simple icing (1 cup powdered sugar whisked with 1 tablespoon milk)
Tiny candies for decorating, such as mini M&M's, mini chocolate chips, white chocolate chips, chocolate and colored sprinkles, coconut flakes, and miniature or crushed candy canes

INSTRUCTIONS

1. Roll out the gingerbread cookie dough on a floured surface. Use the template or your own design to cut out the four sides and two roof pieces for each teeny tiny house you plan to make. Bake the pieces according to the recipe instructions, then let them cool.

2. Assemble the gingerbread house walls using the icing to glue the sections together. Let them dry (for stability), then add the roof pieces. Let them dry again.

3. Decorate the gingerbread houses with icing and small candies. Admire and then eat them.

HEALING CROCK-POT CHICKEN SOUP

Chicken soup is known for its curative powers. Plus it's delicious and comforting and the perfect hot meal on a chilly day, whether you are sick or healthy. This one is made in the slow cooker but can be adapted easily for the stove top.

INGREDIENTS

1–2 boneless, skinless chicken breasts
1 large yellow onion, diced
1–2 leeks, sliced
3–4 carrots, peeled and cut into thirds
3 celery stalks, cut into thirds
1 bay leaf
1 teaspoon dried thyme
3 cloves garlic, minced
2 quart-size boxes chicken stock (or use homemade)
3 cups egg noodles
¼ cup fresh parsley
Salt and pepper to taste
Grandma's Honey-Wheat Bread, to serve (see page 278)

INSTRUCTIONS

1. Place the chicken breasts in the bottom of the Crock-Pot. Top them with the onion, leeks, carrots, celery, bay leaf, thyme, and garlic.
2. Pour the chicken stock over the other ingredients.
3. Put the lid on the pot and cook on low for 6–8 hours.
4. Remove and slice the carrots and celery. Remove the chicken and use two forks to pull it apart. Remove and discard the bay leaf. Add the chicken and the vegetables back to the soup.
5. Add the egg noodles to the soup and stir them in. Put the lid back on and cook on low for another 15 minutes, or until the noodles are soft.
6. Stir in the fresh parsley and salt and pepper to taste. Enjoy a bowl with a slice of Grandma's honey-wheat bread.

GRANDMA'S HONEY-WHEAT BREAD

This recipe is adapted slightly from one passed down to me from my grandma, who clipped the original Granary Bread recipe from the *Cleveland Plain Dealer* newspaper decades ago.

Makes 2 loaves

INGREDIENTS

2 cups all-purpose flour, plus a little extra for kneading
2 packets dry yeast (about 5 teaspoons)
1 tablespoon salt
⅓ cup honey
3 tablespoons butter
2½ cups hot tap water
4 cups white whole wheat flour
½ cup toasted wheat germ (optional)
Butter to grease the pan
Olive or vegetable oil to brush on the loaves

INSTRUCTIONS

1. Combine the all-purpose flour, undissolved yeast, and salt in a large bowl. Add the honey and butter, then the hot water. Mix with a whisk.

2. Add the white whole wheat flour a cup at a time, as well as the optional toasted wheat germ, stirring between each addition.

3. Once you have a soft dough that pulls away from the sides of the bowl, place it on the counter and knead it lightly. (The dough is quite sticky at this point, but resist the urge to add too much additional flour.) Turn the bowl facedown and place it over the bread dough and let it rest for 20 minutes.

4. Punch the dough down and knead it for another couple of minutes. Shape it into two loaves and place them in greased bread pans. Brush

the tops with oil. Cover the loaves loosely with plastic wrap or a damp cloth and refrigerate for 2–4 hours.

5. Let the loaves stand at room temperature while heating the oven to 400°F. Slash the top of the loaves with a sharp knife. Bake 35–40 minutes.

CRUSHED CANDY CANE TOPPING

Crushed candy canes make a tasty and attractive topping to sprinkle over hot chocolate or freshly iced holiday cookies. You can crush the candy canes with a heavy rolling pin, but children really enjoy using a hammer to smash them. A plastic bag helps to keep the candy pieces from flying across the room.

INSTRUCTIONS

1. Unwrap the desired number of candy canes and place them in a resealable, heavy gallon-size plastic bag and seal it.

2. Place the bag of candy canes over a padded surface such as a thick layer of newspapers and let your kids smash the candy canes with a hammer. (*Note:* Do *not* put the bag of candy canes directly on the tabletop, as in the photo shown opposite, unless you want a few dents in your table.)

3. Removed the crushed candy from the plastic bag and store in an airtight container, such as a jelly jar.

4. Sprinkle the crushed candy over hot chocolate, cookies, and cakes throughout the holiday season for flavor and decoration.

PEPPERMINT HOT COCOA

Hot cocoa is a regularly requested beverage in our house during the winter, especially on snow days. Adding a bit of the candy cane peppermint flavor makes it extraspecial.

INGREDIENTS

¼ cup water
5 tablespoons unsweetened cocoa powder
2 cups milk
1 teaspoon vanilla
3 tablespoons honey
1–2 drops peppermint essential oil or ¼ teaspoon peppermint extract
Whipped cream, optional
Crushed Candy Cane Topping (see page 280), optional

INSTRUCTIONS

1. Boil the water in a small heavy-bottom saucepan. Add the cocoa and whisk it to mix it thoroughly. Stir in the remaining ingredients and heat them slowly over medium-low heat (do not boil).

2. Divide the cocoa among cups and add whipped cream and a sprinkle of crushed candy cane if desired.

CANDY CANE LOLLIPOPS

This festive candy is one my children love to make to give as gifts or bring to a holiday party. Almost every step is fun for kids, from arranging the candy canes to adding the sticks and decorating the lollipops with sprinkles and chocolate chips.

INGREDIENTS

Miniature candy canes
Semisweet, milk chocolate, and/or white chocolate chips
Colored sprinkles

INSTRUCTIONS

1. On a parchment-lined baking sheet, assemble two mini candy canes facing each other to form a heart. Slip the end of a lollipop stick between the base of the two candy canes. Repeat to make as many lollipops as desired.

2. Melt the chocolate chips in a double boiler (or in a glass bowl over a pan of simmering water).

3. Spoon the melted chocolate into the heart-shaped space between the candy canes.

4. Add sprinkles and/or contrasting chocolate chips while the chocolate is still soft. Let the lollipops cool and harden.

5. Wrap the candy cane lollipops individually by slipping a small plastic candy bag over the top of each and tying it on with a festive ribbon.

CHOCOLATE-COVERED PEANUT BUTTER BALLS

Every Christmas my aunt Dorothy would send her delicious homemade chocolate bonbons, carefully packaged in an egg carton. This is her recipe.

INGREDIENTS

1 cup chopped nuts
1 cup chopped dates
1 cup creamy peanut butter
1 cup powdered sugar
1 tablespoon butter
1 12-oz. package chocolate chips
6 oz. butterscotch chips

INSTRUCTIONS

1. Mix the nuts and dates together in a food processor until finely processed. Add the peanut butter, powdered sugar, and butter and blend thoroughly.
2. Roll the mixture into 1" balls. Kids love this step, and as you can see from the photos, their peanut butter balls may range in size and shape a bit, which is okay.
3. Melt the chocolate chips and butterscotch chips together in a double boiler.
4. Dip the balls into the melted chocolate and roll them around until they're evenly coated, then place them on a parchment-lined cookie sheet to cool. It will take a few hours for the peanut butter balls to firm up.
5. If desired, you can package these as Aunt Dorothy did, in the sections of a (thoroughly cleaned) plastic or Styrofoam egg carton.

CHERRY HAND PIE HEARTS

Cherry hand pies are delicious anytime, but they're especially perfect for Valentine's Day when you shape them into hearts.

Makes approximately 1 dozen (recipe doubles easily)

INGREDIENTS

1 can (14½ oz.) tart cherries in water; reserve half of the liquid (I buy Oregon Fruit Products found in the canned fruit section of the grocery store, not the baking section; you can also buy them on Amazon.com.)

⅓ cup sugar, plus extra for sprinkling

2 tablespoons cornstarch

⅛ teaspoon almond extract

1 batch Piecrust (see page 142)

Flour for rolling dough

Egg wash (1 egg whisked with 1 tablespoon water)

INSTRUCTIONS

1. Mix the cherries, half of the liquid from the can, the ⅓ cup sugar, cornstarch, and almond extract in a heavy-bottom pan. Cook the mixture over medium heat, stirring regularly, for 8–10 minutes or until the liquid turns thick, gels, and bubbles. Remove the filling from the heat and let it cool.

2. Preheat the oven to 425°F and line two cookie sheets with baking parchment. Also, bring the piecrust dough out of the fridge to soften slightly (about 15 minutes).

4. Divide the piecrust dough into two equal parts and roll out each half separately on a floured surface. Use a 3" heart-shaped cookie cutter to cut hearts out of both pieces of dough. Transfer half of the hearts to the lined cookie sheets.

5. Spoon a couple tablespoons of cherry filling onto the center of each heart.

6. Cover each one with a second dough heart. Press the edges closed with fork tines.

7. Use a sharp knife to cut an X

(for a kiss) in the top crust. (Alternatively, use a tiny heart cookie cutter to punch a heart out of the center of the top crusts before placing them over the filling.) Brush each hand pie with egg wash, then sprinkle them with sugar.

8. Bake for 20 minutes, or until the crust is golden brown at the edges.
9. Enjoy the pies warm or at room temperature.

OATMEAL-CRANBERRY JUMBOS

This, my favorite cookie, is modified slightly from my great-aunt Polly's Oatmeal Jumbos. You can bake these with cranberries, dried cherries, or raisins, as in the original recipe. Make these if you like your oatmeal cookies soft and chewy.

INGREDIENTS

1 generous cup dried cranberries
2¼ cups white whole wheat flour or all-purpose flour, plus a little extra for rolling the dough
1 teaspoon salt
½ teaspoon baking soda
1 teaspoon cinnamon
½ teaspoon nutmeg
⅛ teaspoon cloves
1 cup (2 sticks) butter, softened
1½ cups brown sugar, packed
1 egg
2 tablespoons water
2 cups old-fashioned rolled oats
White sugar, for sprinkling

INSTRUCTIONS

1. Pour boiling water over the cranberries to cover. Let them stand for 10 minutes, then drain.
2. Mix the flour, salt, baking soda, and spices. Add the butter, brown sugar, egg, and water. Work the dough with a wooden spoon until smooth. Stir in the cranberries and oats. Chill the dough for at least 1 hour.
3. Roll the dough out on a floured surface to ¼" thickness. Cut out the cookies with a floured cookie cutter, either heart-shaped, as pictured here, or round. Sprinkle the cookies with sugar.

4. Bake the cookies on ungreased cookie sheets at 375°F for 10–12 minutes. Eat them warm or at room temperature. These are just as good the next day.

Ring In the New Year

After the holiday frenzy there's a whole new year to welcome and plan, combined with some time for reflecting on the year just past. Generally we clean the house from top to bottom, making space for a fresh start, then inaugurate a new calendar and think carefully about our goals and desires. We ring in the New Year as a family with a living room dance party, sparklers, and toasts to each other, letting the kids stay up late (if they can manage it).

OUR FAVORITE BOOKS ABOUT THE NEW YEAR AND CHINESE NEW YEAR

Squirrel's New Year's Resolution by Pat Miller
Shanté Keys and the New Year's Peas by Gail Piernas-Davenport
The Night before New Year's by Natasha Wing
Dragon Dance: A Chinese New Year by Joan Holub
Bringing in the New Year by Grace Lin

SPONGE-PRINTED PERPETUAL CALENDAR

This idea was inspired by and adapted from a calendar by Design Mom. We took her sponge-printing idea and turned her small, monthly watercolor calendar into a larger perpetual calendar that we've used and enjoyed every day since.

MATERIALS

Scissors
Sponge
Paint such as tempera or BioColor in a shallow dish
White poster board

Markers or other drawing materials to decorate the calendar

Transparent contact paper (also called sticky-back plastic), or skip this and just have your poster board laminated, as we did

Wet-erase marker (not dry-erase, unless you opt for the more expensive dry-erase lamination)

INSTRUCTIONS

1. Cut the end off the sponge to make it a square.

2. Press the sponge flat into the paint and then onto the sheet of poster board. Continue making even sponge prints until you have seven squares across and five down. Let the paint dry.

3. Write your child's name or simply "Calendar" at the top. Add the days of the week along the top of the first layer of squares. Decorate the calendar if desired with words, borders, or pictures around the edges. (Don't add dates or months yet.)

4. Cover the surface of the calendar with transparent contact paper or laminate it at a full-service copy shop.

5. Once the calendar is laminated, you can use a wet-erase marker to write the month at the top and fill in the numbers for the days of that month (refer to an online calendar if necessary).

6. Add holidays, events, classes, and appointments for the month, also with the wet-erase marker.

7. Just wipe the calendar clean with a wet sponge or cloth at the end of the month and start again.

WORDS AND WISHES FOR THE NEW YEAR

This fun activity gets the whole family creating together and also thinking about dreams and goals.

MATERIALS

Drawing tools, such as colored pencils or markers
Colored construction paper, cut into triangles
Glue
Collage materials, such as sequins, feathers, decorative papers, and washi tape
Sewing machine
Ribbon (optional)
Hot glue gun (optional)

INSTRUCTIONS

1. Discuss your wishes and goals for the coming year as well as "words for the year," such as *Peace* or *Fun*. Each person can write one or more words on a construction-paper triangle that represent something she or he would like to do, be, or have in the coming year. (Prewriters can dictate their wishes to you.)

2. Each person can decorate his or her triangle as desired, giving life and pizzazz to his or her New Year's wish.

3. Sew the wish triangles together into a bunting using a simple basting stitch (you can add extra scrap-paper triangles in between each as we did, if desired) or glue them to a ribbon with a hot glue gun.

4. Hang the bunting and let your New Year's words and wishes work their magic.

HAPPY NEW YEAR BUNTING

Foil letters make this bunting shimmer and shine both in daylight and by candle-light or holiday lights.

MATERIALS

Sharpie or other permanent marker
Aluminum foil
Scissors
6 sheets of 8½" x 11" white paper
White glue, such as Elmer's
Hot glue gun
Ribbon

INSTRUCTIONS

1. Write "Happy New Year" on the foil in large bubble letters. Cut out each letter.
2. Cut each of the 6 sheets of paper crosswise in half. Glue a foil letter to each half sheet of paper.
3. Use a hot glue gun to glue each bunting section to the ribbon. (Run a thin line of hot glue along the top front of the paper, then press the ribbon faceup over the glue). Leave approximately ½" of space between each paper. I like to make two buntings, one that said HAPPY and a separate one for NEW YEAR, but of course you can create one long bunting instead.
4. Hang the bunting as part of your New Year's decorations and celebrations.

Winter Crafts

> The color of springtime is in the flowers; the color of winter is in the imagination.
>
> —TERRI GUILLEMETS

Winter means snow, of course, at least occasionally in our part of the world, and that is the most anticipated and cherished part of the season for our children. A snow day is a joyous one of stomping and tasting, sledding and frolicking, and making snowmen and snow angels. A snow day also means warming up, back inside the house. It means teddy bear pancakes, hot chocolate, and soup in the Crock-Pot.

In addition to snowmen (and snow women, bunnies, bears . . .), our postholiday winter crafts seem to revolve around the weather: ice sculptures, ice wreaths, and paper snowflakes.

OUR FAVORITE BOOKS ABOUT WINTER

Extra Yarn by Mac Barnett
Annie and the Wild Animals by Jan Brett
Happy Winter by Karen Gundersheimer
The Snowy Day by Ezra Jack Keats
Winter Waits by Lynn Plourde

FOIL SNOWFLAKES

Snowflakes don't have to be made out of paper. Try them with foil instead and then see how they add a cool sparkle to the room.

MATERIALS

Aluminum foil
Scissors
Hot glue gun (optional)
¼" wide ribbon (optional)

INSTRUCTIONS

1. Tear off a square piece of aluminum foil. Fold it in half, then in half again and again (as you would when making a paper snowflake). Round the bottom (opposite the point) with your scissors.
2. Cut out triangles, circles, and snippets along the sides and bottom.
3. Carefully open the snowflake.
4. Repeat to make as many snowflakes as desired, perhaps in different patterns and sizes.
5. To make a garland, use the hot glue gun to attach the foil snowflakes along the ribbon.
6. Use the garland or individual snowflakes as decorations. They are especially beautiful reflecting candlelight or Christmas lights.

COFFEE FILTER SNOWFLAKES

Coffee filters make the best snowflakes. The paper is thin yet tough and (bonus!) already round. They also accept watercolor paint beautifully.

MATERIALS

White bowl-shaped coffee filters
Scissors
Paintbrush (optional)
Watercolor paints (optional)
Newspapers or a mat to protect your work surface (optional)
Glue stick

INSTRUCTIONS

1. Fold your coffee filter in half, then in half again two more times.
2. Make little scissor snips along all of the edges to make your snowflake.
3. If desired, paint the snowflake with watercolors over a protected work surface. Let the snowflakes dry.
4. Hang your coffee filter snowflakes in the window with a dab of glue from a glue stick. (It washes off easily with soap and water when you're ready to remove the snowflakes.)

COLORED-ICE SNOWMAN DECORATIONS

Think beyond the traditional carrot-stick nose and try colored ice shapes to spiff up your snowman this year.

MATERIALS

Ice cube trays, bowls, cake pans, muffin tins
Water
Food coloring or liquid watercolors
Latex or vinyl gloves
String
A snowman or other snow creation

INSTRUCTIONS

1. Fill the bowls, muffin tins, and the like with water. Mix in the food coloring or liquid watercolors. Put the containers in the freezer overnight or leave them outside to freeze if the temperature is low enough.

2. Fill the gloves with water at the tap, add a squirt or two of food coloring, and knot the gloves tight. Freeze the gloves. (*Note:* To make arms for the gloves, insert a stick in the glove of colored water and tie a string tightly around the wrist before freezing.)

3. When you are ready to use your colored ice decorations, set the pans in a sink of warm water just until the ice is loosened enough to come out. Invert the container over a bowl or basin. To remove the gloves from the ice hands, carefully snip and peel them off.

4. Use the colored ice shapes to create eyes, nose, hat, hands, buttons, and other decorations for your snowman.

SNOWMAN PLAYDOUGH SNOW-GLOBE GIFTS

Present playdough molded into a snowman and placed into a "snow globe"—a fun gift for kids to make and to receive!

MATERIALS

1 batch white playdough with silver glitter (see page 16)
Beads
Pipe cleaners cut into 2" and 3" sections
Pint-size mason jars with lids
Labels (see template on page 333)
Glue stick

INSTRUCTIONS

1. Roll the playdough into various-size balls, then stack them to create a snowman approximately 5" tall.
2. Use the beads and pipe cleaner sections to create the snowman's face, arms, buttons, and decorations.
3. Set the snowman on the upside-down lid. Set the mason jar upside down over the snowman and screw it onto the lid.
4. Fill out the gift label and then glue it to the lid.
5. Repeat with as many snowman snow-globe gifts as desired.

STAINED GLASS ICE WREATH

Colored ice makes a fun outdoor wreath for cold winter days (and an interesting one to watch melt on warmer ones).

MATERIALS

Muffin tin, ice cube tray, or cups
Water
Food coloring or liquid watercolors
Bundt pan (or a round cake pan and a plastic cup for the center)
Sturdy ribbon

INSTRUCTIONS

1. Fill the muffin tin or other container with water. Drop food coloring into the sections to dye the water as desired. Put the container in the freezer.

2. Remove the colored ice from the muffin tin by setting it in a sink of warm water briefly to loosen, then invert and arrange it in the bottom of the Bundt pan. (If you're using a cake pan, set the cup in the center first and weigh it down with water.)

3. Pour ice water over the colored ice pieces, just covering them (because you want it to freeze fast). Freeze the wreath. (*Note:* The water needs to be really cold or it will melt the colored ice pieces prematurely. I chill the water first by putting it in a bowl with plain ice cubes.)

4. Unmold the stained glass ice wreath from the Bundt pan by setting it in a sink of warm water for a minute, then turning it upside down over a plate. Tie the ribbon around the ice wreath to hang it or freeze a ribbon loop into the wreath (see step 3 for the Nature Ice Wreath, page 303).

5. Hang your ice wreath outside in the sunlight.

NATURE ICE WREATH

Freeze nature items in wreath form for a lovely outdoor wreath. If you live in a warm climate, you can still make an ice wreath. It'll melt, of course, but that can be interesting to watch.

MATERIALS

Bundt pan (or a round cake pan with a plastic cup for the center)
Nature items such as berries, crab apples, leaves, and flowers
Water
Sturdy ribbon, 8" long

INSTRUCTIONS

1. Fill the base of the Bundt pan with your nature items.
2. Add a layer of water to just cover the nature items. Place the pan in the freezer (or leave outside if it's cold enough) until the water is frozen solid.
3. Make a loop with the ribbon, with the ends inside the Bundt pan and the loop hanging outside the pan, and hold it in place over the edge of the ice wreath while pouring another inch or so of water over the wreath. Place the pan in the freezer again until the water is frozen through.
4. Hang the wreath outside on a tree, fence, or porch and enjoy the sunlight shining through the ice.

PINECONE BIRD TREATS

We love to watch the birds in the winter, whether at our window feeder or at our pinecone bird treats hanging in the trees.

MATERIALS

Spoon or butter knife
Peanut butter
Pinecones
Birdseed (such as sunflower seeds) in a shallow bowl
Scissors
Yarn or string

INSTRUCTIONS

1. Use a spoon or butter knife to spread the peanut butter over the pinecone and into the crevasses.
2. Roll the peanut-butter-covered pinecone in the birdseed to coat it with seeds.
3. Cut 8" lengths of yarn and tie them securely to the stem of the pinecone or around the entire cone, creating a hanging loop.
4. Hang your birdseed treats in the trees for the birds (and the squirrels) to enjoy. Choose a location you can watch from your window if possible.

TISSUE-PAPER CANDLEHOLDERS

Use colorful tissue paper to make these artful candleholders.

MATERIALS

Scissors (optional)
Colored tissue paper (the nonbleeding kind)
Foam brush or regular paintbrush
Mod Podge
Small drinking glasses or votive candleholders
Newspaper or mat to protect your work surface
Tealights

INSTRUCTIONS

1. Tear or cut the colored tissue paper into small pieces. Try hearts, stars, or other shapes if desired.
2. Protect your work surface, then brush Mod Podge over the outside surface of the glass.
3. Press the tissue-paper pieces to the Mod Podge while it is wet, covering the outside of the glass. Brush another layer of Mod Podge over the top of the tissue pieces to make them more translucent and to help them lay flat against the glass. Let the candleholders dry.
4. Place the tealights in your new candleholders and use them to decorate and light the table at your next dinner.

LIGHTED CARDBOARD DOLLHOUSE

Children love to fashion little houses out of cardboard, decorating them with fanciful papers and drawings and adding a string of lights for an extra dose of magic on winter evenings.

MATERIALS

Sturdy cardboard box
Utility knife
Tape
Decorative papers
Markers, for decorating
Glue
Scissors
Transparent contact paper (also called sticky-back plastic)
Colored tissue paper
String of colored holiday lights

INSTRUCTIONS

1. Cut the flaps off two opposing sides of the cardboard box with the utility knife. Tape them to the remaining flaps, then tape the two long flaps together to create a roof.
2. Cut out windows and doors with the utility knife. (My daughter usually draws them on where she wants them, and then I cut them out.)
3. Design your house as desired with decorative papers, markers, drawings, and so forth.
4. Cut pieces of contact paper slightly larger than the windows and larger than one or both of the triangular roof openings. Pull off the paper backing and adhere the contact paper to the inside of the windows with the sticky side facing out. Press small pieces of colored tissue paper against the contact paper to create stained glass windows.
5. Coil a string of colored Christmas lights inside the house and plug them in. Admire the beautiful, lighted dollhouse!

Valentine's Day

With just the right amount of January downtime behind us, for sledding, snow angels, and snuggling up with books, February arrives and then Valentine's Day, a time to celebrate love and friendship in bright reds and pinks. We festoon the house with hearts and bake cookies for ourselves and our friends. We make valentine cards to take to school and mail off to friends and family.

OUR FAVORITE BOOKS ABOUT VALENTINE'S DAY

The Day It Rained Hearts by Felicia Bond
Franklin's Valentines by Paulette Bourgeois
Roses Are Pink, Your Feet Really Stink by Diane deGroat
How Do I Love You? by P. K. Hallinan
If Kisses Were Colors by Janet Lawler

VALENTINE'S DAY SUNCATCHERS

Colorful hearts catching the light in the window—what could be better at Valentine's Day?

MATERIALS

Scissors
Small paper plates
Paintbrush
Watercolor paints
Transparent contact paper (also called sticky-back plastic)
Index dividers made out of translucent colored film, or colored tissue paper
Hole punch
Ribbon or string

INSTRUCTIONS

1. Cut a heart out of the center of the paper plate. Paint the plate with watercolors.

2. Press a square of contact paper to the back of the paper plate so the heart is covered and the sticky side faces the front.

3. Cut the translucent colored index dividers into small pieces. Press them to the sticky contact paper.

4. Use the hole punch to add a hole to the top of the paper plate and string a ribbon through. Hang the suncatcher in a sunny window.

FOIL HEART VALENTINE CARDS

Kids love to try their hand at melted-crayon drawings on aluminum foil. Combine the foil hearts with a message such as "You shine, Valentine."

MATERIALS

Aluminum foil
Cookie sheet (or warming tray)
Towel
Oven mitt or winter mitten
Crayons
Scissors
White glue, such as Elmer's
Blank cards (or paper folded over)
Markers

INSTRUCTIONS

1. Place a sheet of foil on the cookie sheet and heat both in a 350°F oven.
2. Place the hot cookie sheet on a doubled-over towel (to protect the table) and protect the nondominant hand with an oven mitt. Draw and decorate hearts with a crayon on the hot foil. The crayon will melt as you draw, creating vibrant, thick lines (juicy lines, as my daughter calls them). When the cookie sheet cools, just reheat it in the oven and continue.
3. Cut out the hearts from the foil. Glue them to the front of the blank cards.
4. Use markers to decorate the card and write your Valentine's Day greetings and sentiments inside and out.
5. Present a heart to your valentine.

HEART-DOILY-PRINTED T-SHIRT

Wear your heart on your chest with these pretty shirts.

MATERIALS

Spoon(s)

Red, white, or pink fabric paint (I like Jacquard brand; don't use metallic fabric
paint) or BioColor paints mixed with BioColor fabric medium

Acrylic box frame or a flat-bottom baking dish, for rolling out the ink

Mini paint roller (from the hardware store, used for corners and trim in house
painting)

Heart doilies (The stiffer, shinier ones work the best with the fabric paint; the
uncoated kind works best with the BioColors.)

Newspaper and scrap paper

T-shirt

Brayer (hard rubber roller used for printmaking) or rolling pin

Iron

Ironing board

INSTRUCTIONS

1. Place a spoonful or two of fabric paint on an acrylic box frame or on the bottom of an upside-down baking dish. Roll the paint around with the mini paint roller to coat the roller evenly with paint.

2. Lay a heart doily on a sheet of newspaper. Roll the paint-covered roller over the doily to coat the doily evenly with paint.

3. Place the doily, paint side down, on the T- shirt where you want the print. Place a clean sheet of scrap paper or copy paper over the doily and roll over it evenly and firmly with a rubber brayer to transfer the paint to the shirt.

4. Lift the paper and the doily to reveal your heart-doily print. Let the shirt dry overnight.

5. Follow the instructions on the bottle to set the fabric paint

(usually this means ironing it) so that it is colorfast and can be washed and dried normally.

6. Present the T-shirt to a loved one.

VARIATION

If you sew, you can make the doily print on a piece of fabric, trim around the edges, then sew it on a contrasting colored T-shirt as you would an appliqué.

HEART-PRINTED GIFT BAGS

Heart doilies are easily printed onto bags as well as T-shirts, making them perfect for gift giving on Valentine's Day.

MATERIALS

Brown paper grocery bag with handles
Scissors
Sewing machine
Thread in color desired
Spoon(s)
Red, white, or pink tempera paint, BioColor paint, or printer's ink
Acrylic box frame or a flat-bottom baking dish, for rolling out the ink
Mini paint roller (from the hardware store, used for corners and trim in house painting)
Heart doilies
Newspaper and scrap paper
Brayer (hard rubber roller used for printmaking) or rolling pin

INSTRUCTIONS

1. With the brown paper grocery bag folded closed and flat, cut the sides and bottom off, keeping the sections with the handles.
2. You now have two matching grocery bag pieces. Turn them so that the printed sides face each other and the handles line up.
3. Use a sewing machine to sew along the sides and bottom. Use a straight stitch or a decorative stitch with a colorful thread.
4. Following steps 1–4 for the Heart-Doily-Printed T-Shirt (page 312)—but substituting one of the paints listed here for the fabric paint—add a heart-doily print to the bag and let it dry.
5. Slip your gift inside the gift bag (it's the perfect size for a heart-printed T-shirt or a boo-boo heart), and then sew the top of the bag closed if desired.

BOO-BOO HEARTS

For boo-boos, headaches, a sleep aid, and TLC.

MATERIALS

Spoon(s)

Red, white, or pink fabric paint (I like Jacquard brand; don't use metallic fabric paint) or BioColor paint mixed with BioColor fabric medium

Acrylic box frame or a flat-bottom baking dish

Mini paint roller (from the hardware store, used for corners and trim in house painting)

Heart doilies (The stiffer, shinier ones work the best with the fabric paint; the uncoated kind works best with BioColors.)

Newspaper and scrap paper

Muslin or other light cotton fabric in white or natural

Brayer (hard rubber roller used for printmaking) or rolling pin

Iron

Ironing board

Scissors

Pins

White thread

Sewing machine or needle and thread

Millet or rice

Dried lavender (3 tablespoons per cup of millet)

Funnel

INSTRUCTIONS

1. Following steps 1–5 for the Heart-Doily-Printed T-Shirt on page 312, print and set hearts on your white fabric.

2. Once the paint has dried and has been set with an iron, cut out the hearts, leaving a 1" margin around each one.

3. Place two hearts together, face to face, and insert pins to hold them together. Sew them together leaving a ¼" margin around the perimeter of the hearts. Leave a 2" space open along one edge.

4. Turn the heart pillow right side out through the 2" space. Press with an iron.

5. Mix the millet with the dried lavender and, using a funnel, fill the boo-boo heart.

6. Sew the hole up by hand.

7. To use the boo-boo heart, heat it in the microwave or oven for a warming heart or place it in the freezer if you need a cool heart.

MELTED-CRAYON HEARTSTRINGS

These heartstrings combine the symbol of the season with one of our favorite craft projects and look beautiful in a sunny window.

MATERIALS

Cheese grater
Crayons in valentine colors
Bowls or muffin tin
Iron
Wax paper
Ironing board
Newsprint or scrap paper
Scissors
Sewing machine (or see nonsewing option below)

INSTRUCTIONS

1. Follow steps 1–6 of the Melted-Crayon Suncatchers on page 23.
2. Cut the melted-crayon sheets into heart shapes.
3. Sew the hearts together with a basting stitch through the center of the hearts horizontally, leaving an inch or two between hearts. Hang the hearts in a sunny window.

VARIATION

If you prefer not to sew, you can use a hot glue gun to create your heartstrings. Place a dab of hot glue in the center of two hearts and gently run a thread or fine string between the two. Continue by adding more glue dots and hearts.

INTERACTIVE HEART MANDALAS

This back-and-forth game for two or more friends or family members can be a fun Valentine's Day activity (your heart within my heart around your heart . . .) or just a simple drawing game to play while waiting at the doctor's office or restaurant.

MATERIALS

Drawing tools, such as markers or crayons, in a variety of colors
Paper

INSTRUCTIONS

1. The first person starts the heart mandala by drawing a small heart or other symbol in the center of the paper. The second person draws another heart or a different design around the first.

2. The creation of the heart mandala continues as each person adds an additional radiating layer to the design. This can be done either with two people working side by side and taking turns or by circulating the paper around the table in a larger group.

3. Each person can sign the heart mandala when it is deemed finished.

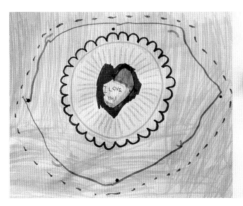 

RIBBON-LACED VALENTINE CARD

This is a great process-oriented valentine activity for younger children. They work on eye-hand coordination and get to use a hole punch (a favorite), all while creating a card for a loved one.

MATERIALS

Scissors

Card stock or watercolor paper

Drawing tools, such as crayons or oil pastels

Paints and paintbrush (optional)

Hole punch (Target sells an inexpensive Up and Up brand paper punch that is especially easy for young kids to use)

Yarn or narrow ribbon

Yarn needle

INSTRUCTIONS

1. Cut the watercolor paper into heart shapes. Punch holes around the perimeter of the heart. (Kids love this step.)
2. Decorate the hearts with drawings, paintings, or words.
3. Thread the needle with yarn or ribbon and let your child use it to sew through the holes in the card. (You may want to tie one end of the yarn through one of the holes first to hold it in place while your child works.)
4. Present to a loved one.

COFFEE FILTER HEART DOILIES

You can make your own heart doilies in much the same way that you make paper snowflakes.

MATERIALS

White bowl-shaped coffee filters
Scissors
Paintbrush
Watercolor paints
Wax paper or a mat to protect your work surface
Glue stick

INSTRUCTIONS

1. Fold your coffee filter in half and cut out a heart along the folded edge.
2. Now fold the heart in half, then in half again two more times, as you would to cut a snowflake.
3. Make little snips along the edges as you would when cutting a paper snowflake.
4. Paint your coffee filter heart doily with watercolor paints over a protected work surface. Let the heart dry. (Or paint and dry before cutting.)
5. Hang your heart doilies in the window with a dab of glue from a glue stick. The glue washes off easily with soap and water when you're ready to remove the doilies.

TISSUE-PAPER HEART-DOILY SUNCATCHERS

Tissue paper suncatchers are given a Valentine's Day twist with these heart doilies.

MATERIALS

Scissors
Tissue paper in valentine colors
Transparent contact paper (also called sticky-back plastic)
String or tape (optional)

INSTRUCTIONS

1. First, cut a symmetrical heart from a sheet of colored tissue paper by folding it in half and cutting a half heart along the folded edge.
2. Fold the heart in half, then in half again (and even again if desired) and make small cuts along the edges as you would to make a snowflake.
3. Cut another heart, somewhat larger than the first, in a contrasting color.
4. Pull the backing off a piece of transparent contact paper. Press the doily heart to the contact paper, then center and press the larger heart over the doily heart. Cut around the heart, leaving a 1" margin of sticky contact paper to use to adhere the suncatcher to the window. (Or if preferred, sandwich the tissue-paper hearts between two sheets of contact paper and hang them in the window with string or tape.)

AFTERWORD

Summer ends, and Autumn comes, and he who would have it
otherwise would have high tide always and a full moon every night;
and thus he would never know the rhythms that are at the heart of life.

— HAL BORLAND

THANK YOU FOR READING! I hope you enjoyed this book and found
some fun seasonal activities to try, decorations to make, and recipes to explore with
your children as you celebrate the seasons and all the beautiful holidays that come
with them.

ACKNOWLEDGMENTS

Thank you to my mother, grandmother, and aunts who have shared their holiday traditions and recipes with me, just as families do around the world.

Thank you to my daughters, who have reignited my love of the holidays and who inspire me to celebrate them artfully. It is a joy to find ways to include them as we explore old traditions and make new ones.

Thank you to all the *Artful Parent* readers who provided their feedback on my very first seasonal-craft e-book.

Thank you to Jennifer Urban-Brown, my editor at Roost Books, whose friendly guidance and professionalism make her a pleasure to work with.

And, finally, a big thank-you to Julie Gibson, my mother and collaborator, whose ability to see both the big picture and the smallest details makes her the best in-family editor a writer could wish for. Her dedication to quality and truth always inspires me.

TEMPLATES

ARTFUL BUNNY EARS TEMPLATE

Enlarge by 200%

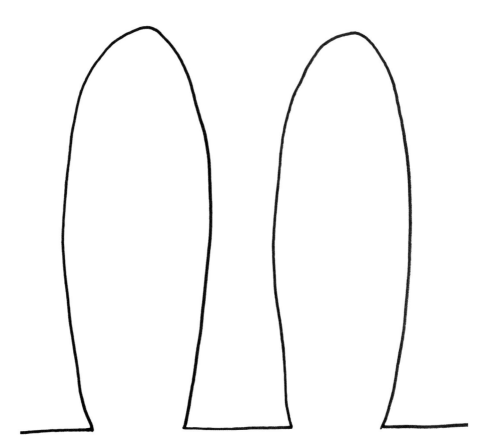

BLUEBIRD PAPER CHAIN TEMPLATE

Actual size

FLOWER CROWN TEMPLATES

Enlarge by 200%

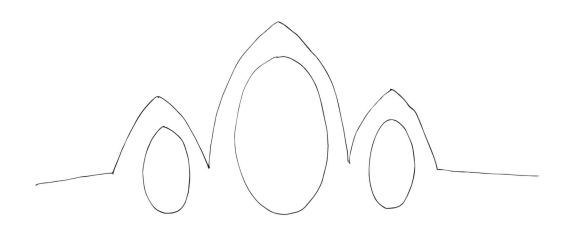

LEAF TEMPLATES

Enlarge by 200%

BAT TEMPLATE

Enlarge by 200%

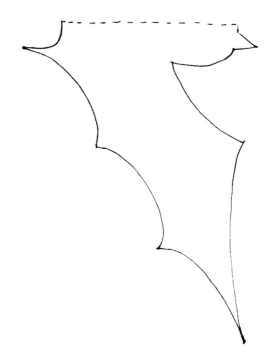

JACK-O'-LANTERN TEMPLATE

Enlarge by 200%

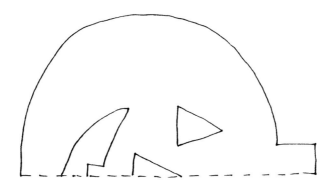

TINY GINGERBREAD HOUSE TEMPLATE

Actual size for the Tiny Gingerbread House
Enlarge by 200% for the Salt-Dough Gingerbread House Lantern

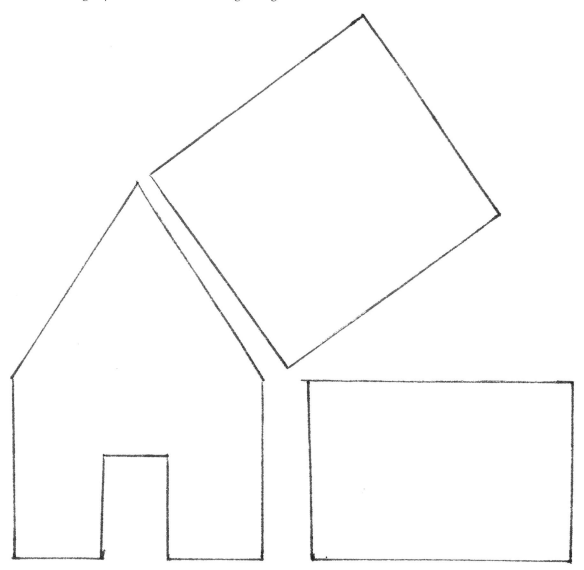

Note: For each, adjust the placement of the door and windows as you like.

CANDY CANE PLAYDOUGH LABEL

Actual size

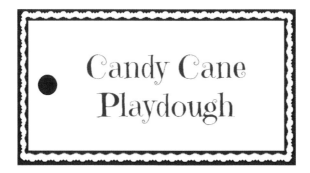

SNOWMAN PLAYDOUGH SNOW-GLOBE LABEL

Actual size

SUGGESTED READING

Seasonal and Holiday Children's Books

Spring
Books about Easter

Brett, Jan. *The Easter Egg*. New York: Putnam Juvenile, 2010.

Friedrich, Priscilla, and Otto Friedrich. *The Easter Bunny That Overslept*. Illustrated by Donald Saaf. New York: HarperCollins, 2002.

Milhous, Katherine. *The Egg Tree*. New York: Aladdin, 1992.

Numeroff, Laura. *Happy Easter, Mouse!* Illustrated by Felicia Bond. New York: Balzer and Bray, 2010.

Tegen, Katherine. *The Story of the Easter Bunny*. Illustrated by Sally Anne Lambert. New York: HarperCollins, 2005.

Tudor, Tasha. *A Tale for Easter*. New York: Simon and Schuster, 2001.

———. *A Time to Keep: The Tasha Tudor Book of Holidays*. New York: Simon and Schuster Books for Young Readers, 1977.

Wells, Rosemary. *Max's Easter Surprise*. New York: Grosset and Dunlap, 2008.

Wing, Natasha. *The Night before Easter*. Illustrated by Kathy Couri. New York: Grosset and Dunlap, 1999.

Zolotow, Charlotte. *The Bunny Who Found Easter*. Illustrated by Helen Craig. New York: Houghton Mifflin, 1987.

Books about Spring

Barklem, Jill. *The Complete Brambly Hedge*. New York: HarperCollins Children's Books, 2011.

Berger, Samantha, and Pamela Chanko. *It's Spring*. Illustrated by Melissa Sweet. New York: Cartwheel Books, 2003.

Beskow, Elsa. *The Flowers' Festival*. Edinburgh: Floris Books, 2010.

Fogliano, Julie. *And Then It's Spring*. Illustrated by Erin Stead. New York: Roaring Brook, 2012.

Hillenbrand, Will. *Spring Is Here*. New York: Holiday House, 2011.

Lewis, Kim. *Little Lamb*. Somerville, Mass.: Candlewick, 2000.

Macken, JoAnn Early. *Waiting Out the Storm*. Illustrated by Susan Gaber. Somerville, Mass.: Candlewick, 2010.

Manushkin, Fran. *How Mama Brought the Spring*. Illustrated by Holly Berry. New York: Dutton Juvenile, 2008.

Martin Jr., Bill, and John Archambault. *Listen to the Rain*. Illustrated by James Endicott. New York: Henry Holt, 1988.

Muller, Gerda. *Spring*. Edinburgh: Floris Books, 2004.

Pfeffer, Wendy. *A New Beginning: Celebrating the Spring Equinox*. Illustrated by Linda Bleck. New York: Dutton Juvenile, 2008.

Plourde, Lynn. *Spring's Sprung*. Illustrated by Greg Couch. New York: Simon and Schuster, 2002.

Ray, Mary Lyn. *Mud*. Illustrated by Lauren Stringer. Orlando, Fla.: First Voyager Books, 2001.

Schnur, Steven. *Spring: An Alphabet Acrostic*. Illustrated by Leslie Evans. New York: Clarion Books, 1999.

Showers, Paul. *The Listening Walk*. Illustrated by Aliki. New York: HarperCollins, 1991.

Books about Gardening

Aston, Diana Hutts. *A Seed Is Sleepy*. Illustrated by Sylvia Long, San Francisco: Chronicle Books, 2007.

Bjork, Cristina. *Linnea's Windowsill Garden*. Illustrated by Lena Anderson. Translated by Joan Sandin. Stockholm: R&S Books, 1988.

Bunting, Eve. *Flower Garden*. Illustrated by Kathryn Hewitt. Orlando, Fla.: Voyager Books, 2000.

Cherry, Lynne. *How Groundhog's Garden Grew*. New York: Blue Sky Press, 2003.

Ehlert, Lois. *Growing Vegetable Soup*. New York: Voyager Books, 1987.

———. *Planting a Rainbow*. New York: Voyager Books, 1988.

French, Vivian. *Yucky Worms*. Illustrated by Jessica Ahlberg. Somerville, Mass.: Candlewick, 2010.

Gibbons, Gail. *From Seed to Plant*. New York: Holiday House, 1993.

Glaser, Linda. *Garbage Helps Our Garden Grow: A Compost Story*. Photographs by Shelley Rotner. Minneapolis: Millbrook, 2010.

Henkes, Kevin. *My Garden*. New York: Greenwillow Books, 2010.

James, Cathy. *The Garden Classroom: Hands-On Activities in Math, Science, Literacy, and Art*. Boston: Roost Books, 2015.

Jordan, Helene J. *How a Seed Grows*. Illustrated by Loretta Krupinski. New York: HarperCollins Children's Books, 1992.

Kudlinski, Kathleen V. *What Do Roots Do?* Illustrated by David Schuppert. New York: Cooper Square, 2007.

Lovejoy, Sharon. *Roots, Shoots, Buckets, and Boots*. New York: Workman Publishing, 1999.

Millard, Glenda. *Isabella's Garden*. Illustrated by Rebecca Cool. Somerville, Mass.: Candlewick, 2012.

Richards, Jean. *A Fruit Is a Suitcase for Seeds*. Illustrated by Anca Hariton. Minneapolis: First Avenue Editions, 2006.

Siddals, Mary McKenna. *Compost Stew: An A to Z Recipe for the Earth*. Illustrated by Ashley Wolff. New York: Tricycle, 2010.

Zoehfeld, Kathleen Weidner. *Secrets of the Garden: Food Chains and the Food Web in Our Backyard*. Illustrated by Priscilla Lamont. New York: Random House Children's Books, 2012.

Books about Birds

Arnosky, Jim. *Crinkleroot's Guide to Knowing the Birds*. New York: Aladdin, 1997.

Aston, Diana Hutts. *An Egg Is Quiet*. Illustrated by Sylvia Long. San Francisco: Chronicle Books, 2006.

Herkert, Barbara. *Birds in Your Backyard*. Nevada City, Calif.: Dawn, 2001.

Rockwell, Anne. *Two Blue Jays*. Illustrated by Megan Halsey. London: Walker Childrens, 2003.

Wellington, Monica. *Riki's Birdhouse*. New York: Dutton Juvenile, 2009.

Books about Butterflies

Aston, Diana Hutts. *A Butterfly Is Patient*. Illllustrated by Sylvia Long. San Francisco: Chronicle Books, 2011.

Heligman, Deborah. *From Caterpillar to Butterfly*. Illustrated by Bari Weissman. New York: HarperCollins, 1996.

Rabe, Tish. *My, Oh My!—A Butterfly! All about Butterflies*. Illustrated by Aristides Ruiz and Joe Mathieu. New York: Random House Books for Young Readers, 2007.

Stewart, Melissa. *A Place for Butterflies*. Illustrated by Higgins Bond. Atlanta: Peachtree Publishers, 2011.

Books about Trees and Arbor Day

Brett, Jan. *The Umbrella*. New York: G. P. Putnam's Sons, 2004.

Cherry, Lynne. *The Great Kapok Tree: A Tale of the Amazon Rain Forest*. Orlando, Fla.: First Voyager Books, 2000.

Codell, Esmé Raji. *Seed by Seed: The Legend and Legacy of John "Appleseed" Chapman*. Illustrated by Lynne Rae Perkins. New York: HarperCollins Children's Books, 2012.

Galbraith, Kathryn O. *Arbor Day Square*. Illustrated by Cyd Moore. Atlanta: Peachtree Publishers, 2010.

Gibbons, Gail. *The Seasons of Arnold's Apple Tree*. New York: Voyager Books, 1988.

Maestro, Betsy. *How Do Apples Grow?* Illustrated by Giulio Maestro. New York: HarperCollins Children's Books, 1992.

Purmell, Ann. *Maple Syrup Season*. Illustrated by Jill Weber. New York: Holiday House, 2008.

Salas, Laura Purdie. *A Leaf Can Be*. Illustrated by Violeta Dabija. Minneapolis: Millbrook, 2012.

Silverstein, Shel. *The Giving Tree*. New York: HarperCollins, 1964.

Books about the Environment and Earth Day

Child, Lauren. *Charlie and Lola: We Are Extremely Very Good Recyclers*. New York: Dial Books for Young Readers, 2009.

Jeffers, Oliver. *The Great Paper Caper*. New York: Philomel Books, 2008.

Okimoto, Jean Davies. *Winston of Churchill: One Bear's Battle against Global Warming*. Illustrated by Jeremiah Trammell. Seattle: Sasquatch Books, 2007.

Showers, Paul. *Where Does the Garbage Go?* Illustrated by Randy Chewning. New York: HarperCollins Children's Books, 1994.

Spinelli, Eileen. *Miss Fox's Class Goes Green*. Illustrated by Anne Kennedy. Morton Grove, Ill.: Albert Whitman, 2009.

Summer
Books about Summer

Beskow, Elsa. *Peter in Blueberry Land*. Edinburgh: Floris Books, 2005.

Carle, Eric. *The Very Lonely Firefly*. New York: Philomel, 1999.

Crews, Nina. *One Hot Summer Day*. New York: Greenwillow Books, 1995.

Dotlich, Rebecca Kai. *Lemonade Sun: And Other Summer Poems*. Illustrated by Jan Gilchrist. Honesdale, Pa.: Wordsong, 2001.

Ehlert, Lois. *Waiting for Wings*. New York: HMH Books for Young Readers, 2001.

Engle, Margarita. *Summer Birds: The Butterflies of Maria Merian*. Illustrated by Julie Paschkis. New York: Henry Holt, 2010.

English, Karen. *Hot Day on Abbott Avenue*. Illustrated by Javaka Steptoe. New York: Clarion Books, 2004.

Franco, Betsy. *Summer Beat*. Illustrated by Charlotte Middleton. New York: Margaret K. McElderry Books, 2007.

Gal, Susan. *Day by Day*. New York: Alfred A. Knopf, 2012.

Gershator, Phillis, and David Gershator. *Summer Is Summer*. Illustrated by Sophie Blackall. New York: Henry Holt, 2006.

Hesse, Karen. *Come On, Rain!* Illustrated by Jon J. Muth. New York: Scholastic, 1999.

Hobbie, Holly. *Toot and Puddle: You Are My Sunshine*. New York: Little, Brown Books for Young Readers, 2010.

Holland, Mary. *Ferdinand Fox's First Summer*. Mount Pleasant, S.C.: Sylvan Dell Publishing, 2013.

Jackson, Ellen. *The Summer Solstice*. Illustrated by Jan Davey Ellis. Brookfield, Conn.: Millbrook, 2001.

Mahy, Margaret. *A Summery Saturday Morning*. Illustrated by Selina Young. New York: Puffin Books, 2000.

McCloskey, Robert. *Blueberries for Sal*. New York: Viking, 1976.

McClure, Nikki. *Mama, Is It Summer Yet?* New York: Abrams Books for Young Readers, 2010.

Meshon, Aaron. *Take Me Out to the Yakyu*. New York: Atheneum Books for Young Readers, 2013.

Muller, Gerda. *Summer*. Edinburgh: Floris Books, 2004.

Nordqvist, Sven. *A Rumpus in the Garden*. Norwalk, Conn.: Opal, 2005.

Ochiltree, Dianne. *It's a Firefly Night*. Illustrated by Betsy Snyder. Maplewood, N.J.: Blue Apple Books, 2013.

Pfeffer, Wendy. *The Longest Day: Celebrating the Summer Solstice*. Illustrated by Linda Bleck. New York: Dutton Juvenile, 2010.

Rocco, John. *Blackout*. New York: Hyperion Books, 2011.

Rylant, Cynthia. *The Relatives Came*. Illustrated by Stephen Gammel. New York: Aladdin, 1985.

Stewart, Sarah. *The Gardener*. Illustrated by David Small. New York: Square Fish, 2007.

Swanson, Susan Marie. *To Be Like the Sun*. Illustrated by Margaret Chodos-Irvine. Orlando, Fla.: Harcourt Books, 2008.

Wilder, Laura Ingalls. *Summertime in the Big Woods*. Illustrated by Renee Graef. New York: HarperCollins, 1996.

Wong, Janet S. *Apple Pie Fourth of July*. Illustrated by Margaret Chodos-Irvine. New York: Harcourt, 2002.

Ziefert, Harriet. *Birdhouse for Rent*. Illustrated by Donald Dreifuss. New York: Houghton Mifflin, 2001.

Zolotow, Charlotte. *The Summer Night*. New York: HarperCollins, 1991.

Books about Adventures and Vacations

Brunelle, Lynn. *Camp Out! The Ultimate Kids' Guide*. Illustrated by Brian Biggs. Technical Illustrations by Elara Tanguy. New York: Workman, 2007.

Donaldson, Julia. *The Snail and the Whale*. Illustrated by Axel Scheffler. New York: Puffin, 2006.

Fleischman, Paul. *Weslandia*. Illustrated by Kevin Hawkes. Somerville, Mass.: Candlewick, 2002.

Frazee, Marla. *A Couple of Boys Have the Best Week Ever*. Orlando, Fla.: Harcourt Books, 2008.

Jessup, Harley. *Grandma Summer*. New York: Viking Juvenile, 1999.

McLerran, Alice. *Roxaboxen*. Illustrated by Barbara Cooney. New York: HarperCollins Children's Books, 1991.

Rey, Margret, and H. A. Rey. *Curious George Goes Camping*. New York: Houghton Mifflin, 1999.

Teague, Mark. *How I Spent My Summer Vacation*. New York: Crown, 1995.

Van Dusen, Chris. *A Camping Spree with Mr. Magee*. Vancouver: Raincoast Books, 2003.

Waldman, Neil. *The Starry Night*. Honesdale, Pa.: Boyds Mills, 1999.

Weitzman, Jacqueline Preiss. *You Can't Take a Balloon into the Metropolitan Museum*. Illustrated by Robin Glasser. New York: Puffin, 2001.

Whitefeather, Willy. *Willy Whitefeather's Outdoor Survival Handbook for Kids*. Lanham, Md.: Roberts Rinehart, 1997.

Books about Water and the Beach

Berkes, Marianne. *Over in the Ocean: In a Coral Reef*. Illustrated by Jeanette Canyon. Nevada City, Calif.: Dawn, 2004.

———. *Seashells by the Seashore*. Illustrated by Robert Noreika. Nevada City, Calif.: Dawn, 2002.

Brown, Margaret Wise. *The Little Island*. Illustrated by Leonard Weisgard. New York: Bantam Doubleday Dell Books for Young Readers, 1973.

Lee, Suzy. *Wave*. San Francisco: Chronicle Books, 2008.

Lester, Alison. *Magic Beach*. Saint Leonards, NSW, Australia: Allen and Unwin, 2006.

Locker, Thomas. *Where the River Begins*. New York: Dial Books, 1984.

London, Jonathan. *Froggy Learns to Swim*. Illustrated by Frank Remkiewicz. New York: Puffin Books, 1995.

McCloskey, Robert. *One Morning in Maine*. New York: Viking, 1980.

———. *Time of Wonder*. New York: Puffin Books, 1989.

Monroe, Mary Alice. *Turtle Summer: A Journal for My Daughter*. Illustrated by Barbara J. Bergwerf. Mount Pleasant, S.C.: Sylvan Dell, 2007.

Roosa, Karen. *Beach Day*. Illustrated by Maggie Smith. New York: Clarion Books, 2001.

Shannon, David. *Jangles: A Big Fish Story*. New York: Blue Sky Press, 2012.

Soman, David, and Jacky Davis. *Ladybug Girl at the Beach*. Illustrated by David Soman. New York: Dial, 2010.

Van Dusen, Chris. *Down to the Sea with Mr. Magee*. San Francisco: Chronicle Books, 2006.

Wiesner, David. *Flotsam*. New York: Clarion Books, 2006.

Zoehfeld, Kathleen Weidner. *What Lives in a Shell?* Illustrated by Helen K. Davie. New York: HarperCollins, 1994.

Zolotow, Charlotte. *The Seashore Book*. Illustrated by Wendell Minor. New York: HarperCollins, 1994.

Autumn
Books about Autumn

Crausaz, Anne. *Seasons*. San Diego: Kane Miller, 2010.

Ehlert, Lois. *Leaf Man*. New York: HMH Books for Young Readers, 2005.

———. *Red Leaf, Yellow Leaf*. Orlando, Fla.: Harcourt Brace, 1991.

Glaser, Linda. *It's Fall!* Illustrated by Susan Swan. Minneapolis: Millbrook, 2001.

Hall, Zoe. *The Apple Pie Tree*. Illustrated by Shari Halpern. New York: Blue Sky Press, 1996.

McNeally, Ranida T. *Our Seasons*. Illustrated by Grace Lin. Watertown, Mass.: Charlesbridge, 2006.

Plourde, Lynn. *Wild Child*. Illustrated by Greg Couch. New York: Simon and Schuster Books for Young Readers, 1999.

Purmell, Ann. *Apple Cider Making Days*. Minneapolis: Millbrook, 2002.

Rawlinson, Julia. *Fletcher and the Falling Leaves*. Illustrated by Tiphanie Beeke. New York: Greenwillow, 2006.

Robbins, Ken. *Autumn Leaves*. New York: Scholastic, 1998.

Spinelli, Eileen. *I Know It's Autumn*. Illustrated by Nancy Hayashi. New York: HarperChildrens, 2004.

Wellington, Monica. *Apple Farmer Annie*. New York: Dutton Children's Books, 2001.

Wiley, Thom. *The Leaves on the Trees*. Illustrated by Andrew Day. New York: Cartwheel Books, 2011.

Ziefert, Harriet. *One Red Apple*. Illustrated by Karla Gudeon. Maplewood, N.J.: Blue Apple Books, 2009.

Books about Halloween

Brown, Margaret Wise. *The Fierce Yellow Pumpkin*. Illustrated by Richard Egielski. New York: HarperCollins, 2003.

Calhoun, Mary. *Wobble the Witch Cat*. Illustrated by Roger Duvoisin. New York: Morrow, 1958.

Carlstrom, Nancy White. *What a Scare, Jesse Bear*. Illustrated by Bruce Degen. New York: Aladdin, 1999.

———. *Who Said Boo? Halloween Poems for the Very Young*. Illustrated by R. W. Alley. New York: Aladdin, 1999.

Donaldson, Julia. *Room on the Broom*. Illustrated by Axel Scheffler. New York: Puffin Books, 2001.

Fleming, Denise. *Pumpkin Eye*. New York: Henry Holt, 2001.

Glassman, Miriam. *Halloweena*. Illustrated by Victoria Roberts. New York: Atheneum Books for Young Readers, 2002.

Hubbell, Will. *Pumpkin Jack*. Park Ridge, Ill.: Albert Whitman, 2000.

Kohara, Kazuno. *Ghosts in the House!* New York: Roaring Brook, 2008.

Moulton, Mark Kimball. *Miss Fiona's Stupendous Pumpkin Pies*. Illustrated by Karen Hillard Crouch. Delafield, Wis.: Lang Books, 2001.

Neitzel, Shirley. *Who Will I Be? A Halloween Rebus Story*. Illustrated by Nancy Winslow Parker. New York: HarperChildrens, 2005.

Roberts, Bethany. *Halloween Mice*. Illustrated by Doug Cushman. New York: Clarion Books, 1995.

Shaw, Nancy E. *Sheep Trick or Treat*. Illustrated by Margot Apple. New York: Houghton Mifflin, 1997.

Silverman, Erica. *Big Pumpkin*. Illustrated by S. D. Schindler. New York: Aladdin, 1992.

Stock, Catherine. *Halloween Monster*. New York: Atheneum, 1990.

Titherington, Jeanne. *Pumpkin Pumpkin*. New York: HarperChildrens, 1986.

White, Linda. *Too Many Pumpkins*. Illustrated by Megan Lloyd. New York: Holiday House, 1997.

Books about Thanksgiving

Child, Lydia Maria. *Over the River and Through the Wood*. Illustrated by Christopher Manson. New York: North-South Books, 1993.

Devlin, Wende and Harry. *Cranberry Thanksgiving*. New York: Aladdin, 1990.

Jackson, Alison. *I Know an Old Lady Who Swallowed a Pie*. Illustrated by Judith Byron Schachner. New York: Puffin Books, 1997.

Johnston, Tony. *10 Fat Turkeys*. Illustrated by Rich Deas. New York: Scholastic, 2009.

Markes, Julie. *Thanks for Thanksgiving*. Illustrated by Doris Barrette. New York: HarperCollins, 2004.

Melmed, Laura Krauss. *The First Thanksgiving Day: A Counting Story*. Illustrated by Mark Buehner. New York: HarperCollins, 2003.

Rylant, Cynthia. *Henry and Mudge under the Yellow Moon*. Illustrated by Suçie Stevenson. New York: Aladdin, 1987.

———. *In November*. Illustrated by Jill Kastner. New York: HMH Books for Young Readers, 2008.

Stock, Catherine. *Thanksgiving Treat*. New York: Aladdin, 1993.

Sutherland, Margaret. *Thanksgiving Is for Giving Thanks*. Illustrated by Sonja Lamut. New York: Grosset and Dunlap, 2000.

Winter
Books about Christmas

Aylesworth, Jim. *The Gingerbread Man*. Illustrated by Barbara McClintock. New York: Scholastic, 1998.

Brett, Jan. *The Twelve Days of Christmas*. New York: Puffin, 1997.

———. *The Wild Christmas Reindeer*. New York: Putnam and Grosset, 1990.

Houston, Gloria. *The Year of the Perfect Christmas Tree: An Appalachian Story*. Illustrated by Barbara Cooney. New York: Puffin Books, 1988.

Isadora, Rachel. *12 Days of Christmas*. New York: Putnam Juvenile, 2010.

Jeffers, Susan. *The Nutcracker*. New York: HarperCollins Children's Books, 2007.

Keats, Ezra Jack. *The Little Drummer Boy*. New York: Puffin Books, 1968.

Mayer, Mercer. *The Little Drummer Mouse*. New York: Dial Books for Young Readers, 2006.

Monroe, Colleen. *A Wish to Be a Christmas Tree*. Illustrated by Michael Glenn Monroe. Ann Arbor: Sleeping Bear, 2004.

Moore, Clement C. *The Night before Christmas*. Philadelphia: Courage Books, 1995.

Parish, Peggy. *Merry Christmas, Amelia Bedelia*. Illustrated by Lynn Sweat. New York: HarperCollins, 1986.

Seuss, Dr. *How the Grinch Stole Christmas*. New York: Random House, 1985.

Slate, Joseph. *What Star Is This?* Illustrated by Alison Jay. New York: G. P. Putnam's Sons, 2005.

Tillman, Nancy. *The Spirit of Christmas*. New York: Feiwel and Friends, 2009.

Vainio, Pirkko. *The Christmas Angel*. Translated by Anthea Bell. Gossau Zürich, Switzerland: North-South Books, 1995.

Van Allsburg, Chris. *The Polar Express*. New York: Houghton Mifflin, 1985.

Waddell, Martin. *Room for a Little One: A Christmas Tale*. Illustrated by Jason Cockcroft. New York: Margaret K. McElderry Books, 2004.

Wells, Rosemary. *Max's Christmas*. New York: Dial Books, 1998.

Wilson, Karma. *Bear Stays Up for Christmas*. Illustrated by Jane Chapman. New York: Margaret K. McElderry Books, 2004.

Books about the New Year

Curtis, Jamie Lee. *My Brave Year of Firsts: Tries, Sighs, and High Fives*. Illustrated by Laura Cornell. New York: HarperCollins, 2012.

Lewis, Paul Owen. *P. Bear's New Year's Party: A Counting Book*. Berkeley: Tricycle, 1989.

Miller, Pat. *Squirrel's New Year's Resolution*. Illustrated by Kathi Ember. Park Ridge, Ill.: Albert Whitman, 2010.

Piernas-Davenport, Gail. *Shanté Keys and the New Year's Peas*. Illustrated by Marion Eldridge. Morton Grove, Ill.: Albert Whitman, 2007.

Wing, Natasha. *The Night before New Year's*. Illustrated by Amy Wummer. New York: Grosset and Dunlap, 2009.

Books about the Chinese New Year

Casey, Dawn. *The Great Race: The Story of the Chinese Zodiac*. Illustrated by Anne Wilson. Cambridge, Mass.: Barefoot Books, 2006.

Chan, Hingman. *Celebrating Chinese New Year: An Activity Book*. Cincinnati: Infini, 2004.

Chinn, Karen. *Sam and the Lucky Money*. Illustrated by Cornelius Van Wright and Ying-Hwa Hu. New York: Lee and Low Books, 1995.

Holub, Joan. *Dragon Dance: A Chinese New Year*. Illustrated by Benrei Huang. New York: Puffin Books, 2003.

Lin, Grace. *Bringing in the New Year*. New York: Dragonfly Books, 2008.

Zucker, Jonny. *Lanterns and Firecrackers: A Chinese New Year Story*. Illustrated by Jan Barger Cohen. Hauppauge, N.Y.: Barron's Educational Series, 2003.

Books about Winter

Bancroft, Henrietta. *Animals in Winter*. Illustrated by Helen K. Davie. New York: HarperCollins Children's Books, 1997.

Barnett, Mac. *Extra Yarn*. Illustrated by Jon Klassen. New York: Balzer and Bray, 2012.

Brett, Jan. *Annie and the Wild Animals*. New York: Houghton Mifflin, 1985.

———. *The Mitten*. New York: G. P. Putnam's Sons, 1989.

Briggs, Raymond. *The Snowman*. New York: Random House, 1978.

Fromental, Jean-Luc. *365 Penguins*. Illustrated by Joelle Jolivet. New York: Abrams Books for Young Readers, 2006.

Frost, Robert. *Stopping by Woods on a Snowy Evening*. Illustrated by Susan Jeffers. New York: Dutton Children's Books, 2001.

Gundersheimer, Karen. *Happy Winter*. New York: Trophy / Harper, 1987.

Judge, Lita. *Red Sled*. New York: Atheneum Books for Young Readers, 2011.

Keats, Ezra Jack. *The Snowy Day*. New York: Puffin, 1976.

Lindgren, Astrid. *The Tomten*. New York: Penguin Putnam Books, 1997.

Martin, Jacqueline Briggs. *Snowflake Bentley*. Illustrated by Mary Azarian. New York: Houghton Mifflin, 1998.

Plourde, Lynn. *Winter Waits.* Illustrated by Greg Couch. New York: Simon and Schuster Books for Young Children, 2001.

Rylant, Cynthia. *Henry and Mudge and the Snowman Plan.* Illustrated by Suçie Stevenson. New York: Aladdin, 2000.

———. *Snow.* Illustrated by Lauren Stringer. Orlando, Fla.: Harcourt, 2008.

Van Laan, Nancy. *When Winter Comes.* Illustrated by Susan Gabor. New York: Atheneum Books for Young Readers, 2000.

Yolen, Jane. *Owl Moon.* Illustrated by John Schoenherr. New York: Philomel Books, 1987.

Books about Valentine's Day

Bond, Felicia. *The Day It Rained Hearts.* New York: HarperCollins, 2006.

Bourgeois, Paulette. *Franklin's Valentines.* Illustrated by Brenda Clark. Tonawanda, N.Y.: Kids Can Press, 1998.

deGroat, Diane. *Roses Are Pink, Your Feet Really Stink.* New York: HarperCollins, 1997.

Hallinan, P. K. *How Do I Love You?* Nashville: Candy Cane Press, 2002.

Lawler, Janet. *If Kisses Were Colors.* Illustrated by Allison Jay. New York: Dial Books for Young Readers, 2003.

Wojtowicz, Jen. *The Boy Who Grew Flowers.* Illustrated by Steve Adams. Cambridge, Mass.: Barefoot Books, 2005.

RESOURCES

The following resources have been carefully selected to provide more information and inspiration as you explore artful family living around the year.

My Art and Craft Supply Picks

Poster Paint

Colorations Simply Washable Tempera Paint (Discount School Supply) for its quality, color, and price. BioColor paint and activity paints (Discount School Supply) for their quality, color, and ability to adhere to a multitude of surfaces without cracking.

Acrylic Paint and Sealer

Reeves Acrylic Paint, Liquitex Basics Acrylic Paint, and Krylon Crystal Clear Acrylic Coating (art supply stores or Amazon.com).

Watercolor Cakes

Lyra, FineTec, or Jolly (Stubby Pencil Studio); Faber-Castell (The Art Pantry); Crayola (drugstore or art supply store).

Liquid Watercolors

Colorations Liquid Watercolor Paint and plastic droppers (Discount School Supply).

Finger Paints

Colorations Washable Finger Paint (Discount School Supply), Crayola Washable Finger Paints (drugstores or art supply stores), or homemade finger paints (see my recipe in *The Artful Parent* or any number of recipes online).

Crayons

Beeswax Crayons, Prang Crayons (made with soy), and Jolly push-up crayons (Stubby Pencil Studio), as well as Crayola Washable Crayons—jumbo for toddlers, thin for older children (drugstores or art supply stores). We also love the novelty of Crayon Rocks (Stubby Pencil Studio) and shaped crayons (Earth Grown Crayons).

Oil Pastels

Colorations Outstanding Oil Pastels (Discount School Supply), Crayola Oil Pastels (art supply stores or Discount School Supply), and Crayola Twistables Slick Stix (art supply stores and drugstores).

Chalk

Melissa and Doug Jumbo Triangular Chalk Sticks (toy stores and art supply stores) for indoor chalkboard use, and Crayola Sidewalk Chalk (drugstores or Target) for outdoor use.

Colored Pencils

Alpino Tri Colored Pencils and Alpino Trimax (chunkier), both with triangular barrels (Stubby Pencil Studio). Art Grip EcoPencils by Faber-Castell are good for older children (Stubby Pencil Studio or Amazon), as are Prismacolor Scholar Colored Pencils (art supply stores).

Markers

Crayola Washable Markers and Crayola Pip-Squeaks Washable Markers (drugstores or art supply stores), and Colorations Washable Markers (Discount School Supply). For permanent markers, we love Sharpie Markers and Sharpie Metallic Markers (drugstores and art supply stores).

Paper for Drawing, Painting, and Collage

Heavyweight white sulphite paper (Discount School Supply), poster board (Target or drugstores), mat board (some frame shops let you take remnants for free), Tru-Ray Sulfite Construction Paper (Discount School Supply), and Mala Paper, assorted colors (Ikea).

Paper for Watercolor Painting

For basic-quality watercolor paper, Canson XL Watercolor Paper (art supply stores), Real Watercolor Paper (Discount School Supply), Strathmore 200 Series Watercolor Pad and Strathmore Kids Paint Pad (art supply stores and Amazon.com).

Paper for the Easel

Easel Paper Roll (Discount School Supply) and Mala drawing paper roll (Ikea).

Paper for Working Big

Brown Contractor's Paper, also known as builder's paper and as paper drop cloth (available at home development stores such as Lowes and Home Depot, near the lumber section) or butcher paper (Discount School Supply or other art supply stores).

Canvas

Stretched canvas and canvas panels come in a wide range of sizes (art supply stores).

Colored Tissue Paper

Colorations Premium Art Tissue Paper—Colorfast (Discount School Supply) or any colored tissue paper (art supply stores, drugstores) and Colorations Premium Art Tissue Paper—Bleeding (Discount School Supply).

Glue

Elmer's Washable School Glue and Elmer's Glue Sticks (drugstores, art supply stores, stationery stores), glue guns (art supply stores), and Mod Podge (art supply stores).

Tape

Colored Masking Tape (Discount School Supply), Blue Painter's Tape (home development stores), and washi tape (CuteTape.com and art supply stores).

Modeling and Sculpture Materials

Playdough (see my recipe on page 16), potter's clay (pottery studios or Discount School Supply), Crayola Model Magic (art supply stores), Sargent Art Sculpt-It Air Dry Clay (art supply stores), wood craft sticks, plaster of Paris (art supply stores), and pipe cleaners (art supply stores).

Paintbrushes

For toddlers, Stubby Chubby Paint Brushes (Discount School Supply) or Melissa and Doug Jumbo Paint Brushes (toy stores or art supply stores). For older children, a variety of sizes and brands found at art supply stores.

Paint and Water Cups

Melissa and Doug Spill-Proof Paint Cups (toy stores or art supply stores) for younger children. Colorations Double-Dip Divided Paint Cups (Discount School Supply), which hold two colors each, for older children who need more color options. Also the smaller 6 Paint Cups in a Base (Discount School Supply) for liquid watercolors.

Art Smock

Make your own from large T-shirts (see instructions in *The Artful Parent*) or just use an old T-shirt.

Art Trays

Use Brawny Tough Large Plastic Art Trays (Discount School Supply) or an old rimmed cookie sheet or plastic serving tray to contain messes. Inexpensive plastic place mats also work well to protect work surfaces.

Glitter

Any glitter from art supply stores; Colorations Glitter Glue and Colorations Washable Glitter Paint (Discount School Supply).

Fabric Crayons, Markers, and Paint

Pentel Fabric Fun Pastel Dye Sticks (Amazon and Dick Blick), Colorations Fabric Markers (Discount School Supply), Jacquard Textile Color (Dharma Trading Company or art supply stores), and BioColor paint mixed with BioColor Fabric Medium (Discount School Supply).

Printing Supplies

Speedball Water-Based Printing Ink, hard rubber brayer, and acrylic box frame—these inexpensive picture frames work well for printmaking (art supply stores).

Liquid Watercolor Paper Leaves (Discount School Supply), Texas Snowflakes (Discount School Supply), paper doilies (art supply stores), embroidery floss and needles (fabric store or craft supply store), pom-poms (craft supply stores), plastic pony beads (Discount School Supply or other craft supply stores), Shrink-It Sheets (Discount School Supply), and translucent colored plastic index dividers (stationery store, drugstore, or Amazon.com).

Places to Buy Art and Craft Supplies (Brick and Mortar)

A. C. Moore (almost everything related to arts and crafts)

Drugstores, including superstores such as Target and Walmart (Crayola, Prang, and other art supplies, including crayons, markers, scissors, glue, poster board, construction paper, and sketchbooks)

Grocery stores (pasta, beans, flour, salt, cornstarch, contact paper, aluminum foil, wax paper, coffee filters, food coloring)

Hardware stores (contractor's paper; wire; wing nuts, bolts, and other items that can be used for collage and sculpture; wood; plaster of Paris)

Ikea (some children's art supplies)

Independent art supply stores (often oriented more toward adults or college students)

Michael's (almost everything related to arts and crafts)

Office supply stores (pens, pencils, stickers, address labels, circle stickers)

School supply stores (more teacher oriented; bulk supplies)

Thrift stores (dishes for paint and art supplies, fabrics, collage trays, old warming trays, salad spinners, muffin tins)

Toy stores (some basic art supplies, such as easels, paint cups, stickers, brushes; many carry Melissa and Doug or Alex brand art supplies)

Online Places to Buy Art and Craft Supplies

Amazon (books as well as many arts and crafts supplies): www.amazon.com

The Art Pantry (children's art supplies): www.theartpantry.com

Artterro (eco-art kits, art journals): www.artterro.com

Bare Books (blank books, puzzles, and games): www.barebooks.com

Cutetape (washi tape): www.cutetape.com

Discount School Supply (almost everything related to arts and crafts, including Colorations brand items, BioColor paints, liquid watercolors, papers, brushes, oil pastels): www.discountschoolsupply.com

Earth Grown Crayons (soy crayons in fun shapes): www.earthgrowncrayons.com

For Small Hands (art supplies, child-size tools and kitchen gear): www.forsmallhands.com

Grasshopper Store (select art supplies and art kits): www.grasshopperstore.com

Imagine Childhood (select art supplies): www.imaginechildhood.com

Stubby Pencil Studio (eco-art supplies, including colored pencils, sketchbooks, markers): www.stubbypencilstudio.com

ABOUT THE AUTHOR

© TIFFANY DAHLE

JEAN VAN'T HUL grew up in eastern Oregon, studied art in New England, and later settled in the Blue Ridge Mountains of North Carolina to raise a family. Her passion for art and creativity has led her to share her ideas for process-oriented art and simple, creative activities with families around the world through her blog and books.